P9-AOT-753

Policy-Making
in
British Government

AN ANALYSIS OF POWER & RATIONALITY

Policy-Making
in
British Government
AN ANALYSIS OF POWER & RATIONALITY

BRIAN SMITH

ROWMAN AND LITTLEFIELD
Totowa, New Jersey

First published in Britain 1976 by Martin Robertson and Company Ltd, 17 Quick Street, London N1 8HL

First published in the United States 1976 by ROWMAN AND LITTLEFIELD, Totowa, New Jersey

ISBN 0-87471-859-7

Typeset by Preface Ltd, Salisbury, Wilts
and printed and bound in Great Britain at
The Pitman Press, Bath

Contents

PART I

CHAPTER 1

Introduction:
The Policy-Making Process

THIS book attempts to bridge the gap between the traditional academic approaches to the study of British government and thereby to relate those approaches to the products of government, namely public policies.

Political science has tended to concentrate on the structure of individual political institutions and the behaviour of the social groups which make up those institutions. It has to some extent been preoccupied with the activities of political organisations and groups in relation to their success in the competition for political power. It rarely sees as one of its primary concerns the contribution which such groups make towards the formation of policy. Yet policies are an important element of the political process, constituting its 'outputs', or the ends to which politics is the means.

Public administration as an academic pursuit has, on the other hand, tended to accept the existence of public policies as given and has concentrated on the machinery for the implementation of those policies. It has attended to the organisation of governmental agencies, the behaviour of public servants and, increasingly, the methods of resource allocation, management and review. From such an approach it is difficult to know much about the way policy is made, although it is generally noted that experience of policy implementation 'feeds back' in a significant way into the policy-making process.

The policy-making process has thus to a large extent been regarded as a 'black box' which converts demands into policies but whose structure is unknown and inaccessible to observation. The study of government has tended to concentrate on the individual parts, or 'structural mechanisms', of the political system without showing how they are related to the end products of the interrelationships. The demands which a society makes on the political system from its economic activities and as a result of its social structure and political

3

culture have been analysed on a comparative basis. How such demands
become translated into political issues, through elections, party and
pressure group activities, political communication and legislative action,
has also been studied, although these aspects of the political system are
often examined in isolation from the policy issues to which they are
related. In studies of voting behaviour, for example, there has been
more interest in the socio-economic and demographic variables relating
to electoral choice, than to the effects of electoral choice on policy
decisions.

The second type of input into the political system — supports —
has also been studied. The supports of a political system consist of
those conventions, customs, rules and assumptions which provide a basis
for the existence of a political community, the regime and the
authorities. There is a substantial literature on the nature of democratic
beliefs in Britain and the doctrines and practices to which they give rise.
More generally political scientists have made many attempts to show
the relationship between such supports and the stability of the political
system as a whole. However they have tended to neglect the
significance of values, rules and conventions for the process of
policy-making.

So far as the political system is regarded as existing to produce
'outputs', or authoritative decisions, these are again often placed at one
remove from public policies. They are at a higher level of generality. In
systems theory they are regarded either as effects on the environment
or as 'feedback' to the political supports of the system (by satisfying
demands to some degree). Outputs are said to constitute a body of
specific inducements for the members of a political system to support
it, either by threats of sanctions, rewards for support given, or by
socialization into the political norms of the society.[1] Studies of public
policy areas (housing, welfare, education, defence and so on), on the
other hand, have tended to neglect the political dimension by
concentrating on the evaluation of policy decisions in terms of specified
values — a rational rather than a political analysis.

The systems approach to political analysis may be depicted by a
diagram, as in figure 1. While appreciating the immense contribution
which systems theory has made to the study of politics[2] it is suggested
that one interesting way of developing this approach is to specify the
interrelationships which link the demands and supports to the
authoritative decisions which all political systems produce. This book
attempts to do this within the context of British government. The

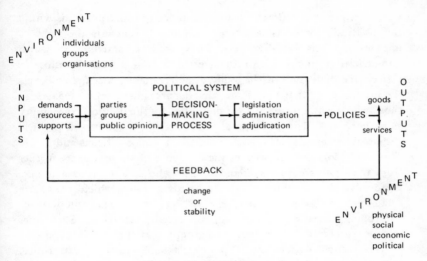

Figure 1: The Political System

primary object is to contribute to the study of British government, but a secondary product may be a methodology which can be applied in other states.

For analytical purposes it is necessary to separate out the interrelated influences and pressures originating in different social groups and the problems which those groups seek to solve, while recognising that the emergence of any single public policy is a highly complex process which in real life does not constitute an identifiable sequence of events which the language of 'ends' and 'means' suggests might exist. Policy-making is 'an extremely complex analytical and political process to which there is no beginning or end, and the boundaries of which are most uncertain'.[3] Somehow a complex set of forces called 'policy-making', taken together, produce effects called 'policies'.

There are two dimensions to the study of policy-making: power and rationality. The first is concerned with explaining how social groups and organisations bring influence to bear on those entitled to take and enforce legally binding decisions. Such decision-makers include those who hold office within the formal or constitutional system of rules which assigns formal powers to various positions within the governmental structure. Politics and policy-making are activities in which people with different values compete for those positions within the political system which confer on their occupants the right to impose decisions on dissenters. They are also activities in which non-official groups seek to influence the decisions made by those in office. One dimension of the study of policy-making attempts to assess the influence of what Lindblom calls the 'proximate' policy-makers, or those who occupy formal offices prescribed by the political community as authoritative. The 'proximate' policy-makers in the British political system are ministers, MPs, local councillors, senior officials and so on. This dimension also investigates the influence of those who are further from the centres of decision-making but who at any given time may perform one or more of the specialised roles which constitute influential behaviour; initiating, vetoing, planning, adjudicating, controlling, moralising, theorising, cooperating, agitating.[4] Such roles may be structured to form organised groups, parties and movements.

The second dimension of policy-making is that of rationality. Despite the limitations on rationality implied by a concept of policy which emphasises the interplay of powerful forces, policy-making is a rational activity in that it involves planning. Policy-making is a combination of politics and planning. It implies intellectual as well as political activity. In government there are many large organisations attempting to impose upon policy-making some of the characteristics of rational thought and action. One of the tasks of the student of government is to investigate to what extent the various decisions which together constitute the formation of public policy are related by rational connections.

There are many ways of specifying what kind of decision-making can be designated rational. One such way is set out in the next chapter as a model to be tested against reality. For the time being, and to indicate the second dimension of policy-making analysis, it is enough to say that so far as public policies are the planned results of decision-making they are arrived at in roughly the following way: a problem is identified; goals or objectives are established; a range of policy options is specified; a choice of the most desirable option is made and this becomes policy. This presentation immediately raises doubts about how far policy-making can and ought to follow this model. It is this problem which the second part of the book discusses.

The study of rationality in policy-making may be seen as the administrative component of government viewed from a new angle. It is within the administration that, for the most part, techniques are continually being developed to improve the capacity of the government for rational decision-making. These techniques, such as cost benefit analysis and output budgeting, will be examined as examples of how governments attempt to improve their decision-making capabilities.

This two-dimensional approach to policy-making makes it possible to bring together parts of the political process which have traditionally been kept apart: politics, involving conflict, power and ideology; and administration, involving analysis, organisation and planning. Alternatively the approach may be said to be concerned with the political function and environment of the administrative process. An approach to British government from the standpoint of power and rationality should relate political and administrative activity to the purpose for which people seek office and influence decisions — the making of public policy.

PLAN OF THE BOOK

The first part of the book deals with the conceptual and theoretical problems relevant to this approach to governmental policy-making. Chapter 2 explores the concepts of policy, power and rationality. 'Policy' is defined so as to reveal the significance of both political values and the methods of decision-making to the end-products of government. Different levels of policy are identified and distinguished from political objectives.

The subject of the book is how policy-makers take decisions. It is therefore concerned with power. Chapter 2 explains the different forms which power can take in the modern state and relates the forms of power to the main elements in the policy-making process. The second dimension to the study of policy-making is rationality. This concept is introduced in Chapter 2 in order to explain how the characteristics of a rational decision-maker and the constraints on rationality must be included in a study of policy-making.

The two dimensions of policy-making can be identified with two theories of government. These are set out in Chapter 3. The first is concerned with the political rules governing the play of power in government. The elements of a theory of legitimate power are elaborated and the basis of consensus explored. This theory provides a setting for the examination of the power of different elements in the political system, and the interrelationships between them, which is carried out in Part II. The theory of government regarded as legitimate by a broad consensus of opinion is explained in terms of the concepts of democracy, representation, majoritarianism, responsibility and devolution. The final concept is important because local government is treated throughout as an integral part of the whole system, providing opportunities for the exercise of power and rationality in policy-making. The exercise of power, through voting and lobbying, for example, has a geographical dimension. Similarly policy-planning exists in local as well as central government. The picture of power-relations in British government is incomplete without a description of relationships between the two levels. This is reserved for a separate chapter, but reference is made in others, where appropriate, to the local community component in power and decision-making.

Chapter 3 also presents a theoretical picture of administrative rationality. Again this is a normative theory in that it describes how a policy-maker would act under ideal circumstances. This chapter is intended as a means to identifying the technical problems of policy-making and as a prelude to the examination of decision-making techniques and the constraints on rationality which the practice of government has to accommodate. It identifies rational policy-making with planning.

Part II examines the interplay of power against the background of the theory of legitimacy. Chapter 4 deals with the power of the individual, first in relation to the significance of voting in the choice of public policies. A number of problems are identified as arising from the view that the choice, through elections, of political leaders can be regarded as a means of influencing policy-making. Group action is usually considered a more effective method than individual action for the ordinary citizen to affect the policies of governments. Chapter 4 examines the motives for pressure group action, the techniques of influence used, and the factors relating to likelihood of success. Finally this chapter examines the mass media as a means of communication between the citizen and the government. If the media can influence opinion in a situation where government is responsive and responsible to the public then they are correspondingly influential in determining policy. This view is considered in the light of evidence about the relationship between the media and the public's political attitudes and actions.

Chapter 5 is concerned with the representative aspects of British government. Since governments at the national level are usually formed by the leaders of the political party with a majority of seats in the House of Commons it is important to know something about the distribution of power in political parties if we wish to know how the parliamentary leadership is likely to behave. Parties are also becoming increasingly significant in local government. Parties seek power nationally and locally by offering the electorate leaders and programmes. An important aspect of the power structure is the way in which leaders are recruited and programmes formulated.

When legislative office has been won, the next stage is to use the power which is legitimised by electoral success. In national government it is widely accepted that Parliament is dominated by the executive in policy-making. Its sovereignty is thought to be real only in a legalistic sense. Chapter 5 explores the relationship between legislature and executive with reference to the power of each and the nature of parliamentary alliances which complicate the picture of simple conflict. The House of Commons is shown as influencing policy-formation in different ways. The factors which affect the alignment of groups within Parliament are examined according to whether they strengthen or weaken the executive. Contrasts are drawn between central and local government.

The executive and power within it are examined in Chapter 6. Particular attention is paid to the collective strength of the Cabinet, the factors contributing to the power of the prime minister and the constraints on him. The administrator's political and policy-making roles are also investigated. The sources of bureaucratic power are examined in both central and local government. The implications of this power for responsible government are explained. The judiciary is also considered as an element in the political process. Chapter 6 considers the impact of judges on policy-making and attitudes towards judicial power in the system of government.

Chapter 7 is devoted to the geographical element in the distribution of political power. It looks at the relationship between the central government and the governments of local communities. The degree of autonomy enjoyed by local authorities is investigated and the pressures for central control explained. The interdependence of central and local government arises from the responsibilities which the central government is given for various aspects of local policy-making and from local government's place in the machinery of government. Central government controls are examined. These controls have given rise to some widespread and influential assumptions about the relationship between the two levels. These are investigated in the light of evidence from recent research into the factors which are related to variations in local policy outputs.

Part III deals with the techniques and approaches to policy-making which attempt to improve the rationality of the process and thereby the efficiency of government policies and programmes. In Chapter 3 it is argued that a model of administrative rationality reveals a need for the specification of functional objectives and the costing of alternative policies linked to them. Chapter 8 describes the budgetary devices used in central and local government to meet these needs — PPBS, corporate planning, public expenditure surveys and programme analysis and review. Emphasis is placed on the technical, organisational and political problems which together limit the technical rationality of policy-making.

Chapter 9 is concerned with the analytical methods available to governments in trying to cope with the problem of uncertainty. Cost-benefit analysis is examined as an aid to rational decision-making when there is no price mechanism to provide efficient resource allocation and the maximisation of welfare. The technical requirements of CBA as a method of making economically efficient choices between different projects are set out. This carries the exposition into related techniques of decision-making provided by operational research. In all cases, however, the emphasis will be on the political significance and practical limitations of these approaches to problem-solving rather than on their technicalities.

Any improvement in the analytical capacity of government demands more and better information. All organisations, and particularly governments, have problems in gathering, processing, interpreting and communicating the technical and political data required by the policy-making process. Chapter 10 examines the different sources of information utilised in British government and assesses their adequacy. It also looks at the organisational requirements of information and applies some of the findings of social psychology on communications to the problem of organising work on policy-planning in government agencies.

The final chapter examines the British power structure by reference to two models of community power: pluralism and the ruling class. The theoretical problems which arise from questions such as, 'who governs?', 'who has power?', 'who influences decisions?' or 'who are the decision-makers?' are explored. The elements of pluralism in British government are set out and an attempt is made to produce a more realistic picture of the power structure by reference to various elitist elements within the system.

CHAPTER 2

Policies, Power and Rationality

Three concepts are clearly fundamental to the study of public policy-making in British government. They have already been used but need some explanation. They are 'policy', 'power' and 'rationality'. Before these concepts are applied to the study of government they must first be explained. They can then be used to formulate and test two theories of decision-making, each of which represents the dimensions of our approach — power and rationality.

POLICY

Sir Charles Cunningham, once permanent under-secretary of state at the Home Office, said: 'Policy is rather like the elephant — you recognise it when you see it but cannot easily define it'.[1] Unfortunately 'it' is something which takes different forms. There is very little advance to be made by designating policy as the 'outputs' of the political system, and even less by defining public policy as 'more or less inter-dependent policies dealing with many different activities'.[2] The magnitude of the problem can be seen from other definitions which have been offered:

the structure or confluence of values and behaviour involving a governmental prescription[3]

decisions giving direction, coherence and continuity to the courses of action for which the decision-making body is responsible[4]

decisions about the goals of the system and the share of the costs that each member, or group of members is expected to pay[5]

general directives on the main lines of action to be followed[6]

changing directives as to how tasks should be interpreted and performed[7]

12

The concept of 'policy' denotes, among other things, deliberate choice of action or inaction, rather than the mere effects of interrelating forces. A policy may lead to an undesirable effect (e.g. mass starvation in Bengal during the Second World War) but such effects are not policies.[8] Outputs must be distinguished from outcomes.

The student of policy-making must be aware that non-decisions are just as important as decisions and policies which initiate some new relationship between government and the governed. Attention should not focus exclusively on decisions which produce change, but must also be sensitive to those which resist change and are difficult to observe because they are not represented in the policy-making process by legislative enactment. Power can be used to prevent decisions and restrict choice as well as to initiate change.[9]

Policies must be distinguished from effects and also from goals or objectives. It may be that good policy analysis in government attempts to clarify goals and objectives, but policies are not selected until this has been done. Policy can be distinguished from objectives as means from ends. It may be, of course that what appear to be ends are in fact means to other ends; and that a means may become an end in itself, regardless of its effectiveness in reaching the objectives for which it was originally designed. All this, however, tells us more about the importance of evaluating the effects of policies in the decision-making process than about the nature of policies themselves which are analytically distinct from the goals which the policy-maker might be pursuing.

If policies are distinct from goals and objectives they nevertheless involve a deliberate choice of actions designed to reach those objectives. The actions referred to can take the form of directives to perform certain actions (for example, pay tax at a certain rate or register a marriage, birth or death), or refrain from certain actions (parking on the wrong side of the street at night or engaging in commercial dealings with Rhodesia). They may take the form of publicly financed services, such as education, health care or housing, or publicly financed projects, such as missiles, power stations or motorways. Policies create obligations for both the citizen (for example, not to develop his land without planning permission) and the state (to provide unemployment benefit to a person who is unemployed, capable of work and available to take a job).

It is clear that within any one policy area (for example, defence or social welfare) there is a hierarchy of policies and a range of different policies. There is, for example, a wide range of benefits paid under social security legislation. Family allowances, welfare milk and foods, retirement pensions and industrial injuries benefits are all policies designed to provide social security. Each has been designated to meet some second-level objective within the very broad goal of 'social security'. The hierarchy of policies develops as rules have to be formulated to govern the various activities which contribute to the implementation of policy. Each policy in the hierarchy corresponds to some value or objective existing at that level. For example, one aim of housing policy is slum clearance. The policy is to give local authorities power to demolish property unfit for human habitation. Within this it is policy to use either clearance orders or compulsory purchase orders. In either case it is policy to require ministerial confirmation. Within the central department there needs to be a policy on what constitutes 'unfitness'. To determine this it is policy to have every house alleged by a local authority to be unfit examined by a housing inspector. In any case of doubt, it is policy to give the owner the benefit.[10] Doubtless there are further rules governing how the inspectors conduct themselves, each reflecting departmental policy on procedures.

Policies thus range from the choice of priorities, through plans, to decision rules.[11] Hence the difficulty in distinguishing policy from administration or policy implementation. What appears to be 'execution by subdecisions' from the level of policy defined as 'general directives on the main lines of action to be followed', may be policy-making itself at a lower level in the organisation, where general policy has to be translated into the more concrete forms needed for administration.[12] The distinction between policy and administration at most reflects nothing more than an artificial dividing-line between 'the broader or narrower, and the more general or more detailed, aspects of governmental decisions'.[13]

Hence also the need to regard policy-making not as an exclusively high-level activity.[14] Moreover the higher-level policy may not be the most significant politically. The Department of Health and Social Security's policy on cohabitation, for example, may be of greater significance than its supplementary benefits policy generally.

The hierarchy of policies corresponds to Simon's distinctions between legislative policy, management policy or working policy. However it is misleading to make too rigid a distinction between factual and ethical questions in policy-making, allocating value decisions on organisational objectives to legislators and factual judgements about the probability of particular actions leading to those objectives to administrators.

In reality policies as much as objectives are chosen under the influence of values. Indeed an objective (such as a properly housed community) may be shared by different political groups; but the means or policies chosen will be dependent on the values of those making the choice. One housing programme will be constrained by an inegalitarian ideology which involves, say, reducing mortgage rates for all, including the wealthy, and the selling of council houses. Another strategy will be equally conditioned by a different evaluation of the side effects of different policy options. Similarly the eradication of poverty may be a widely shared objective, but the policies adopted will be determined by the protagonists' views on the desirability of redistributing wealth.

Policy may be defined as a deliberate course of action or inaction taken by those in office under the influence of values and pressures on the way resources (expenditure and coercion) are to be used in pursuit of objectives or in support of other policies. Public policy is the outcome of decisions about the political allocation of resources and is therefore characterised by the use of legal and coercive sanctions; by being of general concern; and by the application of political values to problem-solving. Austin Ranney has given what is probably the best description of the components of a public policy. It should be added that *public* policies are those adopted and implemented by the governmental authorities, but it is worth quoting in full:

A *particular object or set of objects* — some designated part of the environment (an aspect of the society or physical world) which is intended to be affected.

A *desired course of events* — a particular sequence of behaviour desired in the particular object or set of objects.

A *selected line of action* — a particular set of actions chosen to bring about the desired course of events; in other words, not merely whatever the society happens to be doing toward the set of objects at the moment, but a deliberate selection of one line of action from among several possible lines.

A *declaration of intent* — whether broadcast publicly to all who will listen or communicated secretly to a special few, some statement by the policy-makers as to what they intend to do, how, and why.

An *implementation of intent* — the actions actually undertaken vis-à-vis the particular set of objects in pursuance of the choices and declaration.[15]

Some of the above components of public policy — desired objectives, selected courses of action from among alternatives — clearly imply an attempt at rational decision-making, at linking means to ends. Rationality is the aim of public organisations and needs special elaboration as a concept in the study of public policy-making.

POWER

The idea that policy-making is partly a manifestation of power makes it necessary to consider how power is exercised in the policy-making process. Power implies an ability to bring about some change in the behaviour of other people. In a social context it may be defined as 'the capacity of an individual, or a group of individuals, to modify the conduct of other individuals or groups in the manner which he desires, and to prevent his own being modified in the manner in which he does not'.[16] Power is a particular kind of relationship. It does not exist independently of its use.[17] In terms of public policy the exercise of power means determining the way decisions are made. Such decisions relate to the way individuals are chosen for political office and to the way choices are made between different possible lines of action. They may be electoral decisions, small-group decisions and other forms of collective decision-making involving coalitions and bargaining, or the decisions of significant individuals.

The sources of an ability to effect change in other people's behaviour are many. It is often impossible, in studying policy-making, to identify who had power in the sense of bringing about a crucial change at a significant moment. It is easier to analyse power as an abstract concept than to identify its operation in the complex interrelationships which go to make up the process of public policy-making. It is easier to specify the source of an individual's power than to determine which individuals were powerful in the policy-making process, and why. The problem is compounded by the fact that in politics, groups rather than individuals affect the way policy is made in that even the most 'powerful' leaders depend on others for the support which is a necessary condition of their power.

In policy-making power is exercised by different individuals and groups: the prime minister, back-bench members of the House of Commons, or leaders of organised interests, for example. Each exercise of power constitutes one of the influences which together make up the policy-making process. This is what is meant by saying that there is a 'process' through which public policy is made. The process consists of a sequence of related decisions made under the influence of powerful individuals and groups.

The theoretical analysis of power has differentiated the social relationships through which power is exercised and enables us to distinguish the different types of power involved in policy-making. These correspond very broadly to the groups which take part in the political process.

Office

First, power may have its origins in office. This is what is meant by saying that someone is in authority. Political activity generally is to a great extent concerned with the competition for office and with attempts to occupy those offices of state which confer legitimacy or the right to make certain decisions. Since there are few decisions of any importance which are likely to be taken without consideration of other people's reactions it is better to regard the possession of office (Cabinet minister or, in local government, committee chairman, for example) as providing an opportunity to *initiate* decision-making. An ability to take the initiative in government, rather than merely react to other people's initiatives, is an important source of political power.

The power of initiative derives from what has been called the iron law of oligarchy. This expression was used by the German sociologist Robert Michels to describe what he found in the organisation of overtly democratic bodies, such as the German Social Democratic Party. Michels' research revealed that in large organisations (and this must be particularly true of governments) leaders monopolise power because of their administrative experience, skill and specialisation and the inevitability of delegation from the masses to their leaders. There are many reasons why organisational leaders tend to monopolise decision-making. The net result is to give office-holders a power of initiative which is simply not available to the rank and file: 'The power of determination comes to be considered one of the specific attributes of leadership, and is gradually withdrawn from the masses to be concentrated in the hands of the leaders alone'.[18] It may be an exaggeration to say that office-holders become the sole depositories of all power of initiative, but it is a power which they enjoy more than anyone else even in the most democratic form of government. The nature and form of elitism in British government is something to which we will return in some detail. Associated with the power of decision-making conferred by office is the implied ability to resort to the physical coercion which is at the disposal of the government — what might be called its *de jure* coercive power, backed up by legal force. Political authority means a right to use physical coercion to enforce decisions, as well as the right to take decisions.[19]

Authority in this sense is clearly a special sort of power relationship. It implies legitimacy — that the person in authority has the right to exercise power and that those over whom the power is exercised recognise this right and therefore their own duty to obey. Authority presupposes voluntary obedience.[20] This is the relationship which the German sociologist Max Weber, who probably advanced more than anyone else our understanding of power in politics, called domination.

Obviously there must be reasons why people in some circumstances recognise the exercise of power as right. The feeling that power is legitimate may be engendered in a number of ways. Weber identified three. First, a leader may be endowed with charisma. He then has purely personal qualities, such as heroism, intelligence, magical abilities and oratorical skills, which make his followers recognise it as both right and desirable that they should follow him. Charismatic leaders emerge to meet the demands of circumstance. As soon as the problem of succession has to be solved it is likely that some rules will have to be formulated about the choice of successor. Stability of succession required the 'routinisation' of charisma.[21]

There are then two possibilities suggested by history. One is 'traditionalisation'. Here office-holders and leaders are recruited by appeals to divine authority, by a leader's designation of his own successor, by inheritance or by consecration. The status of leader is then endowed by tradition, not charisma. 'Traditional authority rests on the belief in the sacredness of the social order . . . obedience rests on piety'.[22]

The other alternative is the promulgation of legal rules governing the acquisition of office. Obedience under legal authority is not owed to an individual personally, but to impersonal, abstract rules which specify the rights of office. 'The person in command typically is the "superior" within a functionally defined "competency" or "jurisdiction", and his right to govern is legitimised by enactment'.[23] Authority here is only enjoyed so long as it is confined within the formal legality of the authority's decisions and the scope of its office.

Clearly the third form of domination describes the way in which, in theory, offices and leadership positions are filled in British government. However anyone who has studied politics knows that charisma and tradition are usually present in largely legal systems of domination. Indeed practical experience may show that recruitment according to legal rules is a necessary but not a sufficient condition of exercising power in government. It may be that to be successful in the use of office for political ends a leader will need to have charismatic qualities. Success in the competition for office under legal-rational rules may also be dependent on an ability to meet the requirements of traditional values. To increase one's chances of becoming a Cabinet minister it may be necessary to have been to a major public school. To be a powerful Cabinet minister it may be necessary to have those qualities associated with 'natural' leaders.

Expertise

Political authority is a very complex phenomenon and it is only one source of power in the policy process. The second is that which derives from expertise. To be *an* authority on a particular subject may give one power. Senior administrators and professionals in the service of government are said to enjoy power because of authoritative knowledge which may be based on learning or experience. It may also be necessary, before influence can be effectively exercised by any group in the policy-making process, to demonstrate some authoritative expertise – it is a valuable political resource in the British system of government. Of course there is an important distinction between the authority of an expert, which has power in the sense of leading to an acceptance of his judgement, and the authority of government, which involves the determination of action. But an ability to influence judgement in policy-making may be crucial to the outcome of the process.[24]

The authority of the office-holder, through legitimacy, and the expert, through expertise, is a form of power in that it is causative; it can produce change in behaviour, including decision-making. As we have seen, the political authorities may find it necessary to use another form of power, coercive power. This is a quite distinct form of power in that it does not entail the voluntary obedience of authority. In its purest form it entails the use, or threat, of force.

Coercion and influence

This is the third type of power which must be recognised as existing in governmental policy-making. When applied to the acts of governments in backing up their decisions with the effective use of sanctions it is commonly referred to as just 'power' and carries with it the ideas of finality and irresistibility associated with the concept of coercion. When, however, we turn to the power of groups outside the government we find something which has some of the connotations of coercion, in that threats may be involved. The offer of rewards and the power of persuasion may also be part of the relationship between groups and government. Because of this the term 'influence' rather than 'power' is often used. It has the advantage of suggesting that even where coercion is threatened against the government it is resistible; and that the power of groups may stem as much from persuasion and the promise of rewards as from the threat of punishment. Political influence is characterised by the existence of subordination, as distinct from voluntary and willing compliance, but not complete domination.[25] Power conveys the notion of a capacity to inflict penalties through coercion of a kind usually reserved to the state itself. Influence conveys the notion of inducement and persuasion.[26] The power of the IRA when confronting the police in Northern Ireland is obviously more coercive than the power of the Child Poverty Action Group when confronting the Department of Health and Social Security in London. Yet all such groups have in common the fact that they attempt to use sanctions against those in government. The difference, of course, apart from the legality of their actions, is the resources at their disposal.

The relativity of influence is revealed by the tendency to talk about the *probability* of a policy being different after a group or individual has attempted to exert influence to what it would otherwise have been. To speak of 'attempts' to exert influence also indicates the conditional nature of power in this context. The fact that the amount of influence exerted by a group may vary is further indication.[27] The concept of 'influence' is very useful in the study of policy-making, suggesting as it does a relative rather than an absolute power, and the interplay of competing influences representing the conflicting interests concerned with practically every policy issue.

All the forms of power discussed so far are related to the resources which interests are able to muster in the policy-making process. A group may be authorised to take certain decisions (clinical decisions by NHS doctors, for example). Another group may be regarded as authoritative on a particular matter (the National Institute for Economic Research, for example). It may have coercive power (the IRA in Northern Ireland). The resources may be employed in combination. They may be (and usually are) dependent upon an even more fundamental resource: money. Figure 2 sets out the different types of power, their origins and characteristics, in diagrammatic form.

Successful attempts to exert influence may be based on physical force, as in the *coup d'état* or external aggression. But in the normal run of British government successful influence has its source elsewhere (although 'coercion' may be the label attached to an action by those opposed to it). It will depend on inducements and constraints of a non-physical kind.

Influence or pressure to induce or constrain governmental action takes the form of offering or withholding support for government measures. Support manifests itself in two ways. The first is a willingness to strengthen the political base of the government's power so that, for example, the necessary legislative majorities may be formed during that

Figure 2: Power in policy-making

part of the policy process. Campaign donations may be made and publicity campaigns mounted in an attempt to strengthen the position of the government in the eyes of the public. Favours such as these are offered or threats that they will be withdrawn are made in order to induce or constrain policy decisions.

The second form of support is found in the willingness of influential groups to cooperate with governments in the pursuit of policy objectives. The withdrawal of cooperation may take many forms: sit-ins, resignations from advisory councils, refusals to implement the law (over, for example, the abolition of free school milk or the registration of trade unions under industrial relations legislation), non-cooperation by firms in industrial policy or refusals to participate in consultative procedures.

Policy decisions are taken in the context of overt or latent threats of punishments and promises of rewards which stem from the conflicting demands which sectional interests make on governments. The process is very difficult to analyse, partly because it is often impossible to determine whose influence was critical, and partly because governments sometimes act in anticipation of reactions which, in the event, are not forthcoming. Influence can thus occur without being exerted. It may be necessary to look for 'reactional power', as when a government abandons a course of action because of an adverse reaction which it anticipates in the electorate.[28]

For any specific policy issue it might be possible to measure group influence by, for example, determining the number of office-holders whose behaviour has been changed, the extent to which they have changed their position (in, say, the expenditure of money), the cost to the office-holders in terms of commitment to their previous position, and the range of issues over which the influential group can operate.[29] The problems associated with this are great, not least those of quantifying some of the factors and determining which of two groups is really influential when they both appear to be having success with *some* of their 'targets'. Because of such problems this kind of analysis is probably of more use in clarifying the contrasts between group actions in different political systems than in assigning absolute values to the power of a specified group or organisation.

Despite the problems involved in determining where power resided in a particular policy issue, it is possible to gain some idea of where power resides in a given political system. This is the object of the first half of this book. The idea is not to compare the influence of different groups (in a narrow, pressure group sense) in one issue or across a range of comparable issues. It is rather to broaden the concept of the influential group to include all the social groupings involved in politics, to show what groups are active or likely to be active at any given time, and to reveal the factors relating to the likelihood of them exerting some influence on policy-making. We will begin by setting up a model of the system, in this case set out in terms of British constitutional theory, since such theories prescribe the processes by which offices are filled and political decisions are made and, in so doing, represent a conception of political power. This theory will then be examined in the light of what we know about power relationships between and within different political groups and institutions in British government. The results of this investigation should not only allow the theory to be put to the test, but also throw some light on another classic problem in the study of politics: the nature of elitism in British government and the concept of a ruling class.

RATIONALITY

The concept of rationality must be employed in the analysis of government since all the organisations concerned directly or indirectly with government — parties, pressure groups, cabinets, even legislatures and particularly executive departments — attempt to utilise the resources at their disposal to achieve specified tasks or goals. They may be more or less successful in relating means to ends. Their rationality may be limited so that they *'satisfice* because they have not the wits to *maximise'*.[30] Most of the discussion of rationality in government later in this book is about such limitations. Nevertheless the organisations of politics, and especially those which constitute the machinery of the state, attempt to arrive at rational decisions in the pursuit of their objectives.

This book is in part concerned with rationality in administrative organisations. This is not because it is assumed that non-administrative bodies, such as pressure groups and political parties, are irrational organisations. Such an assumption would be false. Organisations of this kind are just as keen as government departments to devise the most appropriate means of achieving what they perceive as desirable goals. They may employ the same techniques of analysis and decision-making (although the analytical resources at their disposal will often be less than those available to the state). The study of rationality in British government focuses on administrative organisations because the community expects these to be effective in planning, on behalf of and subject to the control of political leadership, courses of action affecting the whole of that community. If we demand planning we demand rationality; and it is to the administration that these demands are directed.

Planning is thus the administrative part of the policy-making process. It is an activity for which we depend on permanent officials organised for the purpose. Planning 'is that activity that concerns itself with proposals for the future, with the evaluation of alternative proposals, and with the methods by which these proposals may be achieved'.[31] It is a rational process determining the framework of future decisions. Most tests of a good organisation would include the existence and adequacy of its planning machinery.

Planning in the sense used here obviously has nothing to do with the extent of government intervention in economic and social affairs, although it is often falsely assumed to imply a high degree of state control. Planning does not refer to any specific objective, as in economic planning. Even the most devout believer in limited government would require the state's minimal functions to be performed with rationality. To that extent the services provided by the state, however few, must be planned.

Similarly planning is by no means exclusively the responsibility of those at the highest levels in an organisation. It goes on at different levels. We often talk about planning the implementation of policy, as if planning followed from the choice of policy objectives and was therefore the concern exclusively of line managers. While planning in this sense is an obviously important aspect of organisational activity, it tends to imply a distinction between policy and administration which is no longer considered viable. However, there is some value in distinguishing between the planning of objectives, long-range planning or policy-planning; and the planning of organisational activity in order to achieve the desired policy results.

Policy-planning requires decision and choice which is as far as possible self-conscious, deliberate and rational.[32] 'Behaviour is purposive in so far as it is guided by general goals or objectives; it is rational in so far as it selects alternatives which are conducive to the achievement of the previously selected goals'.[33] The planning of public policy, like all rational behaviour, employs efficiency as its main criterion of choice. It searches for the quickest and cheapest route to its goals.[34] Herbert Simon defined efficiency as a fundamental principle of administration: 'Among several alternatives involving the same expenditure the one should always be selected which leads to the greatest accomplishment of administrative objectives; and among several alternatives that lead to the same accomplishment the one should be selected which involves the least expenditure'.[35] Administrative organisations use this criterion in both the planning and review of administrative activities. The political culture demands that administrative organisations should emulate economic man in maximising the attainment of ends with scarce resources.

This explanation of planning and rationality in administrative organisations may appear to imply that what are supposed to be agencies set up to carry into action the decisions of society's elected representatives and political leaders are in fact major participants in the process of defining society's goals and selecting the appropriate means to those ends. Such a conclusion is inescapable as will be shown later in the chapter on the role of paid officials, or bureaucrats. Administrative power is part of the price which a modern society pays for efficient administration. The modern state seems to be characterised by the delegation or even abdication of power — from the individual to groups, from legislatures to executives, from communities to their represent-atives, from rank and file to leaders. This is no less true of the relationship between political executives and their administrative servants. The administrative organs of the state have as great a role to play in formulating policy as in implementing it. For this reason society, through the political system, is likely to be as concerned with ensuring the efficiency and rationality of the administrative process as with controlling bureaucracy's political power, if not more so. The following chapter attempts to set out a model of rational decision-making as applied to the formulation of public policy. Later on the elements of this model are related to the techniques of policy-planning at present being developed in government agencies. An examination of these techniques provides ample illustration of the constraints on rationality which exist in all decision-making situations and especially in government.

CHAPTER 3

Political Rules and Administrative Reason

THE purpose of this book is not merely to describe the interplay of numerous political forces in the formation of policy, but also to explore the structure of power in British politics in the light of our democratic ideals. To achieve these two ends it is necessary to state the ideal systems of power and decision-making which the dominant values in our society create. Those ideals or theories may then be compared with reality and any divergencies noted and, hopefully, explained. This chapter presents the first stage of the operation. It sets out the elements of democratic theory as they relate to the distribution of power in British government. It also provides a model of rationality relevant to decision-making for the purpose of policy-formation in government organisations. It will be the task of subsequent chapters to test these theories of power and rationality by reference to the actual operation of power and decision-making in British government.

A THEORY OF LEGITIMATE POWER

Without wishing to beg the question of whether the British system of government is pluralistic, and therefore consists of roughly equal competing elements, or elitist, with some elements more powerful than others, it is useful to regard policy-making as having some of the characteristics of a game. Like games, the policy-making process is rule-bound.[1] In British government the relevant rules controlling the 'play of power' are found partly in the constitution and partly in those aspects of the political culture which prescribe how political activity should be carried on. The second set of rules may be less explicit than those embodied in the constitution but they nevertheless regulate the policy-making process.

Constitutional rules specify how those in authority are to be recruited and how they are to use their official positions in making decisions. They are rules which govern the governors by providing a 'framework of norms and practices which define and regularise the management of political relationships'.[2] They consist of laws, customs and conventions which enable us to recognise offices and decisions as authoritative.

Since, as we have seen, authority is dependent on the values of those who respect it, it follows that constitutions are founded on fundamental beliefs about how relationships between government and the governed are to be judged in ethical terms. Such a set of beliefs, values, perceptions and emotions is known as the political culture. Only by reference to it can we explain why constitutions endure of fail.[3]

As far as the rules governing the play of power are concerned, however, they are to be found in parts of the political culture which extend beyond that which supports the constitution or regime to encompass our perception of the political community as a whole and its legitimate boundaries. It also provides us with normative standards for evaluating the performance of government. These standards are by no means applied uniformly by all sectors of British society. Society is divided in the way in which it evaluates the legitimacy of the state's territorial jurisdiction, the rightful access of certain types of people to political roles or the extent of state intervention in social and economic affairs. Nationalism, women's liberation and the free enterprise movement are clear evidence of this. The political culture is a dynamic force. Variation in the balance of opinion and the strength of political values produces change in the scope of government policy-making and in the rules of the political game. Any analysis of public opinion as a factor influencing policy decisions or policy processes must take opinion at this most fundamental level into account.

The first of the two dimensions of policy-making is power. The first model, then, which is needed is a theory of legitimate power in British government which can be tested by reference to reality. This is no easy task since there is considerable disagreement among the experts not only on how the constitution actually works but on how it ought to work. The unwritten nature of the constitution and the difficulties created by the uncertain status of conventions make authoritative interpretation difficult. However it is possible to construct a theory of legitimate power by combining cultural values and constitutional rules in a way which gives a fair representation of what most people would regard as a democratic system of government in the British context. It should then be possible to estimate how far such democratic ideals are realised in practice and to what extent elitism obstructs the realisation of democratic goals.

The theory of legitimate power can be broken down into the following elements.

i Democracy   The British system of government purports to be democratic. This requires it to ensure that the wishes of the people are reflected in the decisions of governments. There are two essential requirements, according to Dorothy Pickles, which must be fulfilled if a system of government is to be democratic. 'It must, first, be able to elicit as accurately as possible the opinion of as many people as possible on who shall be their representatives and on how the country ought to be governed. Second, it must provide ways of ensuring that those chosen by the public do in fact do what the electorate wants them to do or that they can be replaced if they do not, even between elections'.[4] Democracy, then, means representative and responsive government.

ii Representation   Direct democracy being impossible, representative democracy is the next best thing. It entails the free choice of representatives by all adults through fair elections. 'In western democracies representation by election has come to be regarded as the most important form of representation, and indeed the only proper basis of a political system'.[5] In Britain it is important to note that the representative quality of members of Parliament owes more to their manner of selection than to their subsequent behaviour. They are not expected to act as delegates or agents of their constituents. However manner of selection does not denote all that is involved in being an elected representative. 'It would seem that elected persons can be described as representatives only if their election involves some obligation, however slight, to advance the interests and opinions of their electors'.[6] In representative democracy it is assumed that the practice of submitting certain office-holders to periodic re-election will ensure that attention is paid to the interests of those who are represented. In this sense the people may be said to be politically sovereign, transmitting their will effectively to the government. The people initiate the process of legislation and policy-making by voting for candidates whose opinions, values and intentions they know and understand.

Representation, however, carries with it the clear implication of delegation from the people to a legislative body. In Britain Parliament exercises supreme legal power. The government is dependent on the support of the legislature for its existence. Through Parliament the representatives of the people frame laws and decide policy by majority vote.

iii Majoritarian government Since people are divided on who they want to represent them and the decisions that should be arrived at in determining public policy, some method has to be devised to resolve conflict. The democratic method is the majority decision.

Majoritarianism in decision-making (including decisions to choose leaders or representatives) is adopted because the alternatives would be authoritarian. Majority decision is a convenience when values are assigned equal weights. It is not a question of majorities being 'right' and minorities 'wrong'. 'The majority is a shifting aggregate of interests, and its only claim to prevail is that it is more numerous, not that it is more virtuous'.[7] Majority rule therefore presupposes the equal ability of everyone to form part of the majority. It also presupposes the rights of a minority to attempt to become a majority.

Such rights are shored up by the political equality implied in 'one man, one vote' and by the basic freedoms which are said to protect the rights of minorities — of speech, of publication and of association in political organisations. 'Opposition must be regarded as being no less legitimate than power.'[8] They are also supported by the rule of law which prescribes that those in authority shall be as subject to the laws as those who are not, thus preventing any abuse of the powers which derive from a majority position. The rule of law further guards against the tyranny of the majority by providing for an impartial judiciary which will arbitrate free from any bias towards the interests of the authorities.

iv Responsible government Effective government requires the appointment of office-holders whose responsibility it is to implement the laws. It is a necessary condition of British democracy that the executive should be accountable to the elected representatives of the people. In Britain the responsibility of government may also be judged according to its responsiveness to public opinion and its ability to avoid irresponsible action — imprudence and inconsistency.[9] The link between representative and responsible government is to be found in the fact that the accountability of the executive to the legislature ensures that the government is both responsive and respectable.[10]

Responsibility in Britain refers to both the collective actions of the government and the acts or omissions of individual ministers and their departments. Governments are required to answer to Parliament and resign if their policies prove unacceptable, thus losing them the confidence of the legislature. Individual responsibility requires ministers to answer for their own conduct and the conduct of their departments. If found culpable they should resign from office.

Government implies administration and the employment of paid officials organised for effective and efficient work in executive departments. Responsible government is designed to prevent democracy from falling prey to bureaucracy in the sense of government by officials. Responsible government presupposes that politicians, not officials, receive the praise and blame for executive action. The officials remain the anonymous and loyal servants of the government, neutral in their political outlook and recruited on the basis of merit, a qualification which excludes ideological predisposition and therefore patronage.[11]

v Local democracy   This is an element of our political system which is often ignored in discussions of constitutional and cultural rules. Yet it is surely of some constitutional significance that the administration of many services at the local level is in the hands of local *governments* and not local *officials*. It is of cultural significance that we tend to regard local democracy and the administration of services by elected representatives as embodying higher values than those of other forms of local administration (field administration, for example).

The constitutional place of local authorities is signified by the fact that they are the creations of Parliament. They owe their powers, their territories, their status, their very existence to statutes passed by Parliament. The form of decentralisation which they represent is thus devolution, not federalism. It is Parliament which decides to create local elected councils, which devolves the power to exercise a limited discretion in the administration of specified services to them, which defines their territorial jurisdiction and which permits them to tax. Power is allocated between central and local government by the former, not by the constitution as in a federal state. It is allocated by a simple act of Parliament.

The place of local government in the political culture is reflected in the values which are thought to attach to local self-government as a form of administration. The accountability and control of local officials is best enforced by local elected assemblies and not through the remote central legislature. Local democratic institutions provide vital opportunities for political education through participation. Local democracy, in theory, ensures the responsiveness of administration to the peculiar interests of local communities, and protects the general health of democracy.[12]

The theory of legitimate power thus has a geographical dimension which is as important an area of exploration as the 'play of power' among social, economic and political groups. It will therefore be necessary to examine the real, as distinct from the theoretical, relationship between local and central government in Britain to see what degree of power is devolved to localities and what form it takes.

vi Consensus A distinguishing feature of the British political culture is thought to be the level of consensus which supports the values outlined above. Despite a quite considerable consciousness of class differences in British society, it is argued, there is widespread agreement about the basic rules of political life. The British political system is thought to be one of the most stable in the world. Consensus is said to exist on the desirable nature, pace and method of social and economic change. Fundamental differences seem to go no further than different interpretations of the British Constitution — the 'Liberal' versus the 'Whitehall' model.[13] There is little questioning of the fundamental principles of the economy and polity.[14]

Professor Finer similarly emphasises the stability of a regime founded on the 'homogeneous and politically consensual nature of British society'.[15] A lack of profound ideological disputes about the nature of society and the economy and the existence of a relatively high level of confidence in and respect for British political arrangements has led to both substantive and procedural consensus. Neither religion, nationalism nor class threatens this consensus. The prominence given to class in British politics is explained by the absence of other conflicts and not by its own divisiveness.

In another book Finer groups Britain among countries with a 'mature political culture'. In such countries there is wide public support for the procedures for transferring power and for the legitimacy of existing centres of power: 'Public involvement in and attachment to these civil institutions is strong and widespread'.[16] There is a strong belief that any exercise or transfer of power in breach of these procedures would be illegitimate and therefore lacking any moral right to be obeyed.

What is the source of this consensus and consequent stability? How is it that class, regional and other cleavages do not constitute a threat to political stability? Why is there so little apparent dissatisfaction with the socio-economic substance and political procedures of the *status quo*? The causes are much more difficult to identify than the effects.

Almond and Verba, in their survey of attitudes pertaining to the political cultures of different democratic states, found that in the United States and Britain there was both commitment to the political system and trust in the political elite: 'The sense of trust in the political elite — the belief that they are not alien and extractive forces, but part of the same political community — makes citizens willing to turn power over to them'.[17] Almond and Verba also suggest that the attitudes of trust and cooperation frequently expressed by their British respondents reduce commitment to political groups and movements which are against the system: 'These general social attitudes temper the extent to which emotional commitment to a particular political subgroup leads to political fragmentation ... this sense of community over and above political differences, keeps the affective attachments to political groups from challenging the stability of the system'.[18]

Conclusions such as these imply that the stability of a democratic system of government depends on the extent to which those who are governed regard it as fair and just. Inequalities will be tolerated so long as they appear as a consequence of scarcity and not discrimination. If conflict is resolved in 'a spirit of impartiality'[19] consensus is likely to be strong. If the rules of the game seem to be permanently biased in favour of some sections of society at the expense of others, consensus will be weakened. While those in a minority feel that decisions are arrived at fairly and that they have some hope of reversing them by constituting part of the majority themselves, the system will be respected. If, on the other hand, they feel continually discriminated against, their support for the system will dissolve. Consensus and stability are therefore to be explained by the existence of a system of government which does not identify itself with one interest to the exclusion of all others. John Stuart Mill may have been over-optimistic when he wrote: 'We need not suppose that when power resides in an exclusive class, that class will knowingly and deliberately sacrifice the other classes to themselves.' But he was surely right in saying that 'In the absence of its natural defenders, the interest of the excluded is always in danger of being overlooked.'[20] For Mill the superiority of representative government rested upon the principle 'that the rights and interests of every or any person are only secure from being disregarded when the person interested is himself able, and habitually disposed, to stand up for them'.[21] We might conclude that consensus is vulnerable and stability threatened whenever some interest, whether it be economic, regional or religious, feels that despite the existence of formal political rights and liberties it is perpetually excluded by the nature of the regime from fair treatment. A system of government which in moral terms is right may in sociological terms be the only kind likely to survive.

A number of different sets of political actors can be identified from the theory of legitimate power outlined above: the public, the groups into which it divides to reflect its interests, the mass media, elected representatives, political parties, ministers, paid officials, judges, local councils. Each set of political actors must be examined in detail to see how they are related to the process of policy-making — to see who has power and under what circumstances it is exercised. It will then be possible to see how far reality departs from the democratic model and just what kind of elitism we are left with.

A THEORY OF ADMINISTRATIVE RATIONALITY

Modern governments have come increasingly to expect that their administrative organisations will provide the analytical capability necessary for the planning of government policies. Techniques are being developed which assist administrators and politicians in the appraisal of plans and the review of past performance. In so doing they bring about greater rationality in the process of decision-making involved in the choice and execution of public policy. This section sets out a model of the decision-making process appropriate for the governmental policy-maker as a prelude to later consideration of the tools of analysis available, their strengths and weaknesses. What follows is a model in the sense of an ideal type rather than a deductive theory. It presents a picture of an abstraction rather than reality. The elements of the abstraction represent extreme values and may be used as standards of comparison with actual entities. It is usual to refer to the sets of decisions occurring in policy-making as 'stages', implying some historical ordering of events. This is perhaps inevitable for analytic purposes but should not obscure the fact that in real organisational life the different sets of decisions give rise to information which continually feeds into every other set.

An idealised version of the policy-planning process may be represented as having the following stages or sets of decisions.

i Identifying the problem   The policy-maker first identifies a problem or situation in the community which requires action and for which there is no existing policy or set of rules. More often there will be a policy which is applied to a related field but which is inadequate for the new problem which has occurred. For example, existing energy policy may be inadequate to cope with a massive increase in the price of imported oil. Because of the effects on the balance of payments new policies may be required to reduce demand through savings at home, such as a loan scheme for energy-saving investment in industry or a weighting of price increases to deter consumption by the private motorist rather than industry.

Implicit in the definition of a problem or identification of a situation is recognition of the need to act. Such recognition may be created by one set of values while another will perceive the problem differently or will not consider one exists at all. Problems do not 'occur'. They are man-made, created by the application of values by decision-makers to situations. The immigration of Kenya Asians to Britain produced a 'problem' for the race-conscious, but not for non-racialists. Or rather the problem was perceived differently: how to keep them out by the first group; how to integrate them smoothly by the second.

The identification of a situation needing action or the absence of a problem both imply the choice of an objective. Traffic congestion or accident 'black spots' by definition imply the objectives of smooth flows and road safety. The problem of terrorism implies the objective of deterrence. The objective of reducing the proportion of our national income spent on defence follows from the identification of present levels of defence expenditure as a problem. The identification of problems and the concomitant setting of objectives provides the motivation and impetus for the subsequent decision stages in policy-making.

This stage of the policy-making process is characterised by the conflict of values. It is highly charged politically, revealing the impact of contrasting ideologies on policy-making. Fundamental values are brought to bear on society. Indeed, it is a principle of democracy that all values should be respected and provided with opportunities for expression.

None of this should be taken to mean that this stage of policy-making is strictly to do with ethics, not facts. The consideration of social consequences is never entirely absent even from the most abstract discussion of political values. It may be that values are dominant in the establishment of political ends or goals, and rationality is dominant in decisions about means. However the choice of means is rarely a totally neutral exercise, and the choice of ends may involve many assumptions about present and future states which depend upon factual calculations for their reasonableness. In policy-making value judgements need to be made explicit and information on their consistency and consequences fully explored.[22]

ii Alternative strategies   There will usually be a number of alternative courses of action open to the policy-maker to achieve his ends. Limitations on choice have already been established by the decision-maker's perception of the problem, but alternatives are still available. The main task of the planner at this stage, however, is to become aware of the constraints on his freedom of choice. This is what Friend and Jessop refer to as the 'context of operations'.[23] It consists of on-going or operational policies, the availability of resources and the objectives of the planners.

Here then is the interface between 'stages' *i* and *ii*. It establishes the 'opportunity area', or 'all of those acts or courses of action which the effectuating organisation is not precluded from taking because of some limiting condition'.[24] The values of the planner and of other groups are brought into play so as to restrict the range of actions open. For example, housing policy-making is constrained by values relating to public and private ownership, the availability of money and materials, and existing policies regarding building standards and methods of financing housing projects. Nevertheless a pure rationality model of decision-making presupposes a complete inventory of the possible alternatives.

This is an aspect of the pure rationality model which has been subject to severe criticism. It is usually pointed out that it demands the impossible. There are too many alternatives to be considered in the time usually available, even if the creativity, initiative, knowledge, energy and willingness were there, which they are not.[25] Hence the creation of alternative theories of decision-making, such as the 'satisficing', 'incremental' and 'optimal'. These will be referred to again when this stage of policy-making is examined with reference to British government. Now it will suffice to note that the policy-maker must find solutions to his problem 'in circumstances where the range of possible solutions is not easily enumerated, and where it may be difficult either to discover any feasible solution at all, or to be sure that certain significant alternatives will not remain undiscovered'.[26] Yet this stage is a necessary condition for the preference which has to be expressed and the choice of future action which has to be made.

iii Predicting consequences   This stage involves calculating the costs and benefits of each alternative policy option. The determination of consequences is necessary before a rational choice of alternative can be made. For each alternative it is necessary to predict what the consequence or outcome will be and to calculate what the probability is of that consequence occurring.[27] Where it is possible to assign probabilities to the occurrence of an event risk is involved. Where it is not there is uncertainty or subjective probability.

The concept of subjective probability implies the discretionary element which enters into decision-making under conditions unfavourable to the calculation of probabilities. 'Selection of strategies under uncertainty conditions requires the application of judgement, opinion, belief, subjective estimates of the situation, plus whatever objective data is available.'[28] Uncertainty is reduced by the accumulation of information. At this stage, therefore, the decision-maker seeks to add information to take him away from ignorance, through uncertainty, towards known outcomes with assignable probabilities (risk) and, eventually, certainty. The cost of collecting information must also enter into the cost-benefit analysis of alternative strategies.

The information needed to reduce uncertainty in policy-making is of three basic types.[29] First there is uncertainty about the external environment of the policy-maker. Uncertainties here relate to the structure of that environment and change in it. The predictability of demand for higher education is a case in point. Uncertainties of this kind are usually reduced by research into the social, economic and physical attributes of the community. Such research may involve surveys and predictive models. It may be very expensive.

The second type of uncertainty in government is about other areas of policy-making which impinge on the problem under consideration. Future intentions in 'related fields of choice'[30] must be taken into account. It is precisely this uncertainty which leads to demands for better coordination in government, whether it be between, say, the social services and housing departments of a local authority in relation to families in need, or at Cabinet level in attempts to formulate a comprehensive strategy for government policy.

Thirdly, there are uncertainties about the appropriate values to be brought to bear on a problem. Value judgements have to be made about the possible outcomes of different courses of action. Uncertainties of this kind are essentially political and can only be reduced by the dominance of a group or by compromise and bargaining between conflicting pressures. Hence the need to recognise that policy-making does not form a unilinear process: the values which determine the policy-makers' perceptions at stage i are a factor in the reduction of uncertainty at stage iii.

iv Policy selection   Having ranked alternative policies and their consequences in order of preference the rational policy-maker chooses the highest. Here the problem is that of 'expressing preferences between alternative solutions given only imperfect information as to the range, scale and value of their anticipated effects'.[31] In principle the decision-maker's task is to compare the consequences of the policies he has enumerated with his objectives and choose the one which most closely matches those objectives. The best alternative is that which reaches the objective with least cost or provides more objectives for the same cost. Thus a housing policy which clears slums *and* preserves valued kinship structures will be preferable to one which only clears slums unless the cheapness of the latter outweighs the benefits of the former.

The choice of policy involves commitment to a course of action. Such a course of action is usually designated a 'programme'. Friend and Jessop distinguish policy and programmes, both being the products of this stage of policy-making, in the following way: 'a *programme* as a set of related future intentions in respect of certain *specific* situations which are anticipated in the future, and a *policy* as a set of future intentions in relation to certain *classes* of situation'.[32] A programme is thus policy operationalised.

v Review   Policies, unlike decisions, require ongoing activities. Their rationality therefore includes a post-decision stage, namely review. Policy-makers are expected to compare the results of policy-execution with their earlier expectations. The object of the exercise is to explain and evaluate deviations. This stage has other functions than the pursuit of efficiency. In government efficiency has only developed relatively recently as an objective. Originally the task of review was that of the traditional audit: to see that there had been no misappropriation of funds or illegal spending.

POLICY-MAKING AS PLANNING

The components of a rational decision-making system, when applied to governmental policy-making, constitute a process of planning: 'Any process of choice will become a process of planning (or strategic choice) if the selection of current actions is made only after a formulation and comparison of possible solutions over a wider field of decision relating to certain anticipated as well as current situations.'[33] Policy is planned so far as choices of executive action are based on a statement of objectives and an evaluation of the effects of policies designed to achieve them. The process of rational policy-planning may be represented in diagrammatic form as in figure 3, which is a modified version of the very helpful diagrammatic representation of decision-making in local government to be found in Friend and Jessop's *Local Government and Strategic Choice*.

It should be clear from the stages into which the policy-making process can be broken down that different types of information and analysis are required to improve rationality and efficiency. First, a situation or problem in the community has to be perceived and appraised. Judgements have to be made in terms of values. The dominance of values is for the political system to decide on, subject to whatever other relevant information may be forthcoming from the other activities required by the policy-making process. Part II of this book is concerned with the deployment of power in the determination of dominant values.

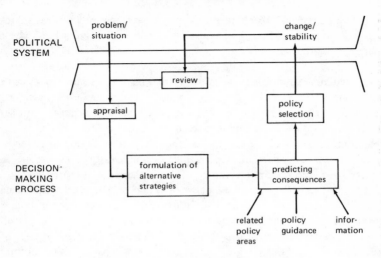

Figure 3: *The policy process*

Secondly, there is a need for objectives and the alternative courses of action leading to them to be clearly specified and carefully costed. Government agencies must be aware of what they are currently buying and what alternative patterns of expenditure might buy for them. This requirement applies to all the action programmes which make a particular policy operational. In performing this analytic function the government planner provides valuable information for the perception and evaluation stage by developing quantitative specifications of community needs. By specifying objectives in quantitative and qualitative terms it makes them measurable and therefore more easily comparable. Output budgeting or planning-programming-budgeting systems (PPBS) is a set of techniques and approaches to policy-making which is central to rational planning. It attempts to specify the total financial cost of a particular objective by calculating the cost-effectiveness of alternative strategies. At least, this is the aim of PPBS. How close it comes to achieving it in British government is the subject of a later chapter.

Thirdly, there is the problem of predicting the probable consequences of different courses of action, consequences which extend beyond the purely financial. The policy-maker requires as complete a picture as possible of the costs and benefits of different courses of action. This picture can then be set against political values and pressures in selecting the course of action which gives the highest margin of benefits over costs.

A particular need at this stage of policy-making is for some quantitative weighting to be given to costs and benefits which cannot be assigned values by the price mechanism. Also the side effects of different courses of action need to be taken into account. Cost-benefit analysis is the technique increasingly used at this stage of policy-making in order to reduce uncertainty, establish probabilities and clarify risks. Its use in government, and the limitations on it, are explained in Chapter 9.

Finally, at all stages in policy-making, as in decision-making generally, there is a need for information. Discerning problems, formulating solutions, deciding on preferences, reducing uncertainty all require useful information. There are many different types of information relevant to government, but new analytical techniques make increasingly heavy demands on the available supply and when available it has to be communicated to those who need it. There are many problems to be faced in British government in the gathering and communication of information for policy-making (see Chapter 10).

PART II

CHAPTER 4

Individuals, Groups and the Media

THE CITIZEN AS POLICY-MAKER

The logical place to begin an investigation of political power in a democracy would seem to be the individual citizen. A democratic form of government is supposed to reflect the will of the people. Yet neither the 'citizen' nor 'the people' is a particularly satisfactory concept for analysing political power. Acting alone, the individual citizen of a state of some fifty million people is rarely a significant political force. The public or the people, on the other hand, suggests a unity of will, purpose and interest which does not exist. There are many publics expressing different and often conflicting values and interests. If the individual acquires power it is likely to be as a member of a group.

The significance of the individual citizen is further reduced by the fact that power in a representative system of government is delegated to a relatively small group of office-holders. They may be controlled and held accountable for their actions. Nevertheless government is an activity reserved by necessity for the few. For the majority of people political action constitutes a very small proportion of their total range of social activities.

Furthermore it would seem that the majority of those who become involved in politics prefer to do so on an individual, *ad hoc* basis, rather than form some enduring relationship with a political organisation. The Civic Culture survey found that of those who felt that they could do something about a regulation which they considered unjust (78 per cent in the case of local government regulations and 62 per cent for national regulations) the great majority would either act alone, by contacting political leaders and administrative officials or by voting, for example (41 per cent) or act through an informally organised group (26 per cent). Only 5 per cent declared they would join a party or pressure group. On this evidence continuous political activity is not regarded as particularly attractive even to those who feel themselves politically competent.[1]

Only a small minority hold legislative office in central and local government — about 24,500. An even smaller proportion occupy executive and judicial offices. Admittedly the public services employ large numbers of people who are directly occupied by the business of government — about 6.5 millions if we include the police, teachers, the Health Service and the nationalised industries. However, we can safely assume that only a very small minority are in a position to influence the choice of public policies and these leading, powerful officials constitute a very small percentage of the working population.

When we move outside the scope of government offices and look at different types of political activists we again find that politics has attractions for relatively few people. Butler and Stokes estimated that only 0.3 per cent of the electorate hold some local party office, that 3 per cent campaign at general elections and 8 per cent attend political meetings during election campaigns. Some 14 per cent are estimated to subscribe to a local party and 25 per cent of the electorate are nominal party members. One of the most interesting findings of the Civic Culture survey was that only 25 per cent of the respondents thought that the ordinary man should be active in local government and politics.[2] Some organisations which get involved in politics (like trade unions and employers' organisations) are not necessarily exclusively concerned with it. Even within those that are (such as political parties) it is important to remember that the leadership is more likely to be influential than the rank-and-file members, a factor which again reduces the political significance of the 'average' citizen.

ELECTORAL CHOICE

For the majority of adult citizens the act of voting constitutes the sole form of active political participation (leaving aside the 92 per cent in the Butler and Stokes sample who followed the 1964 general election campaign via the mass media or by personal conversations). On average since the war approximately 77 per cent of the electorate have voted in national elections (the percentage for local elections is much lower as is discussed later). How far does the act of making an electoral choice constitute an exercise of citizen influence in the selection of public policies?

On the face of it voting would seem to be a most significant and decisive act, leading to the formation of legislative majorities with clearly delineated programmes. Elections are opportunities for citizens to choose between alternative policies offered by candidates for governmental office. 'The meaning of representative government is,' according to John Stuart Mill, 'that the whole people, or some numerous portion of them, exercise through deputies periodically elected by themselves the ultimate controlling power, which, in every constitution, must reside somewhere. This ultimate power they must possess in all its completeness. They must be masters, whenever they please, of all the operations of government.'[3] Yet when we look at the reality of electoral situations such a theory of citizen power, at least in regard to the determination of public policy, must be qualified in many respects.

In the first place elections perform many other functions than the democratic selection of policy options. Some of these are related to the eventual selection of policies. Some are very remote from it indeed. In Britain it is now widely accepted that elections involve the choice of political leaders. The electorate's choice is more a question of who governs rather than how they govern. Such a choice may be seen by the voter as between groups of politicians or simply two or three party leaders. The alternatives are rival elites rather than rival legislative programmes. The other functions of elections are that they provide a peaceful means of solving the problem of political succession. They may help to reinforce the legitimacy of the regime. They may be an educative force. They provide ritualistic opportunities for the citizen to exercise his rights (if not his power).[4]

Secondly, electoral choice is expressed as a vote for a political party. It must not be forgotten that the parties fight the campaign very largely in terms of policies and legislative intentions. The voter sees his role in terms of party. The parties give meaning to politics in the mind of the electorate. They are identified by the voter with the broad goals and objectives which he seeks through the medium of government. 'Whatever the degree of its ignorance or confusion, the electorate attempts to use the ballot to achieve things it cares about.'[5]

What is significant about these 'things' is that they are desired results expressed in very broad terms — ends rather than means, goals rather than policies: 'The public tends to focus on certain conditions or values of which it has more direct experience, rather than attempting the more complex assessment of means and ends which in some form must enter the Government's choice among alternative policies.'[6] The electorate expect the party they vote for, if elected to office, to do certain things. They assume that if things go wrong it is the fault of the governing party. Elections thus enable the electorate to punish or reward the government party for its past performance. However the voter is less concerned with the means of producing desired results, in terms of economic prosperity, peace, justice or social welfare. He or she may well be mistaken in or ignorant of the causal relationship between government policies and desired goals. Elections, then, rarely depend upon issues of policy.[7]

Thirdly, even when policies and political issues elicit strong feelings on the part of electors and are clearly identified with the philosophies and programmes of the political parties, other conditions have to be met before they will affect the electoral strength of political parties and so constitute an exercise of popular sovereignty. In the first place the issue must be important to a substantial proportion of the electorate. Next, issues must not divide the country evenly if they are to affect the strength of the parties. Opinions must not only be strongly felt and widespread, they 'must be skewed rather than equally balanced'.[8] The electorate must also be able to differentiate between the parties in terms of the issue. 'Unless one party or the other is more closely linked to the values or policies which give the issue content for most electors, the issue cannot shift the balance of party strength, however strongly formed and skewed the opinion it excites.'[9] Issues vary widely in the extent to which they exhibit these properties. In the judgement of Butler and Stokes the majority of issues at the time of a general election fail even the first test.

Fourthly, the party images to which the public respond are made up of many elements which bear little relation to policy choices. How people associate parties with the things they value clearly forms an important part of these images. But so do their perceptions of the links between class and party, of their 'modernity' and of the experience, intelligence, sincerity and other personal qualities of party leaders. This is not to deny of course that these elements in a party's image may be regarded as instrumental in the achievement of valued goals and therefore indirectly related to the process of policy choice. Indeed Birch argues that: 'The general image of each party which is of such crucial importance is itself built up by a continuous debate, inside and outside Parliament, over questions of policy, as well as by the success or otherwise of the governments' actions.'[10] Moreover to support a party for very general reasons, such as because it is perceived as being the party of the voter's class, is to choose policies, if only in the sense of tacitly endorsing whatever policies a group of leaders cares to adopt.

Fifthly, another factor which is said to minimise the significance of the voter in the choice of policies is his general lack of knowledge about, or interest in, political issues. This is not to say that voters are to a large extent irrational; the use of this derogatory term in electoral situations is often based on serious misconceptions of the nature of electoral choice.[11] It is to say that there are many determinants of voting behaviour — class, age, religion, region, sex and so on — which are more important than the comparative evaluation of party programmes. There is now a large body of convincing evidence which suggests that the majority of voters are ill-informed about political issues. Attitudes on many issues are non-existent and the ability to differentiate between the parties in terms of party goals or characteristics is poorly developed. Most students of electoral behaviour would now agree with Butler and Stokes that: 'The limits of the public's overt political behaviour are matched by the limits of its political information.'[12] This judgement would seem to apply equally to knowledge of political issues, the identity of political leaders and the structure and process of government generally. Furthermore the crucial 'floating voters', on whose behaviour election results depend, tend to be less interested in and informed about political issues and personalities than the two-thirds of the electorate who are committed to the two major parties.

In view of this it is not surprising that electors lend their voting power to parties whose policies they do not entirely approve of. The degree of acceptance by voters of their party's policies is surprisingly low.[13] Interestingly it is not so much that people do not know what the parties stand for, as that their own attitudes do not correlate with party beliefs. This is even the case with party activists. There is thus little consistency in the partisan attitudes of voters. People do not consistently adopt right- or left-wing attitudes over a whole range of issues on which the parties differ. Butler and Stokes concluded from their survey data that: 'There could be few more forceful comments on the limited extent to which party orientations reach down into the mass public, or on the limited role which tightly clustered policy beliefs play in the motives for party work.'[14] This phenomenon is further reflected in the fact that the electorate does not appear to see politics in terms of a single left–right ideological dimension.[15]

Power and the electoral system

The configuration of electoral power is further complicated by the effects of the electoral system. In the first place the voter is being asked to register decisions on all manner of policy issues through a single vote. In the absence of proportional representation, referenda (the Common Market referendum of 1975 being the sole exception), nominating conventions, primaries and other means of formally registering a choice he has to make do with a single, simple decision as to whom among a small handful of candidates in one of 650 constituencies he should support. As voters, individuals have no say in the choice of candidates for election, the choice of leaders for party office, or the choice of issues for decision. To become involved in these choices they must become party activists, a role which only a tiny minority is prepared to take on.

Then again it is possible for election results to be significantly influenced by abstention — by those who make no choice other than to stay at home. Butler and Stokes have shown how the electoral fortunes of the two major parties between 1959 and 1966 were affected by differential turnout, although in estimating its effects this variable cannot be isolated from the simple conversion of party support, the physical replacement of the electorate and votes for the minor parties.[16]

A further element in the electoral system which must be taken into account when assessing the power which elections give to the individual citizen is the effect of single-member constituencies combined with the simple-majority method of securing election. The principle of political equality implicit in the rule 'one man, one vote' also requires that one vote equals one value. Yet the electoral system makes some votes more valuable than others. The fact that only a simple majority is needed to win a constituency means that the parties inevitably accumulate 'unnecessary' votes. If these are not equally distributed between the parties then it can be argued that the party which needs the smallest number of votes on average to win constituencies has a greater proportion of 'effective' votes.

Unequal representation is also brought about by the uneven population size of constituencies. Boundary changes tend to lag behind population changes. Scotland, Wales and Northern Ireland are, for political reasons, given a guaranteed number of constituencies regardless of population. There is also the need to make constituency boundaries correspond to local authority boundaries. If there was absolute equality of population size the sparsely populated rural constituencies would be too large geographically. So again the effectiveness of the vote varies according to the average number which a party requires to win a seat.

Then there is the fact that under the simple-majority system the distribution of parliamentary seats among the parties, where one seat represents one constituency, need not be, and is unlikely to be, proportionate to the distribution of votes between the parties. Indeed a party may have a minority of votes but a majority of seats. Smaller parties under this system are usually underrepresented. The results of the two general elections in 1974 illustrate this.

Party share of votes and seats

	February 1974		October 1974	
	% votes	% seats	% votes	% seats
Conservatives	38.1	46.6	35.8	43.5
Labour	37.2	47.4	39.3	50.2
Liberal	19.3	2.2	18.3	2.0
Others	5.4	3.8	6.6	4.3

The question then arises: are not some votes more equal than others when a party supporter's vote is worth more than another, when a Scottish, Welsh or Northern Irish vote is worth more than an English, and when the majority voting against the successful candidate in a constituency have no representative of their choice? How the answer to this question is regarded depends on whether it is believed that the power of the voter is more important than the power of the government; and whether the voter's power is likely to be significantly increased by allowing elections to produce legislatures which are more representative of society in the sense of statistically mirroring political attitudes. Against the view that the present electoral system produces unrepresentative assemblies it can be argued that a more proportionate system would give rise to all the uncertainties associated with coalition governments over which the power of the individual voter would be even further reduced. It is much more difficult for the voter to hold parties accountable at elections when responsibility is diffused among the members of a coalition.[17]

Electoral strategy and policy choice

Electoral power presupposes that the different sets of policies offered by parties and leaders at election time will be translated into corresponding decisions once office has been won. Yet the correspondence of policy outputs to electoral intentions is by no means always so close. First, circumstances outside the control of a government may force it to take decisions which its election pledges suggest it would not otherwise have taken. *Force majeure* becomes stronger than *vox populi* and election pledges are abandoned. An alternative effect of this is to require decisions which formed no part of electoral statements of intention and which therefore have received no endorsement by the electorate. For example the financial collapse of Rolls-Royce forced the 1970—74 Conservative administration to abandon its policy of withholding state aid from 'lame ducks', presumably because of the intolerable unemployment situation which would have resulted from the pursuit of this policy. More recently massive increases in the world prices of basic commodities, particularly oil, have influenced practically every policy decision which governments have had to take.

Secondly, a party may adopt rash electioneering tactics only to find to their embarrassment that their promises are impossible to carry out. The Conservatives' promise in 1970 to 'reduce prices at a stroke' was an electoral success which produced a failure of policy.

Thirdly, policy intentions may be thwarted by administrative complications. It is often very difficult to tell whether such complications are real, even with the best administrative will in the world, or whether they have had to face administrative obstruction. An example of genuine practical impossibility was the payment of increased pensions and social security benefits after the general election in March 1974. The Secretary of State for Social Services had to admit that 'such was my desire to get the pension increases paid as quickly as possible that I did not think sufficiently about the effect this would have on the social security staff who had to perform this massive up-rating job'.[18]

Fourthly, a government's legislative programme may be overtaken by political events so that a policy fails to survive a general election. This happened to the 1964—70 Labour administration's plans for a comprehensive state pension scheme which failed to get through the necessary parliamentary stages before the government was voted out of office.

Finally, when in office a party often gives relatively low priority to its major electoral pledges and only a small proportion of legislation is based on them. Manifesto pledges may figure largely in the early stages of a new government's legislative programme but other sources of policy initiative rapidly exceed electoral promises in importance. Not all policy-making requires legislation but whether it does or not, only a minority of policies during the lifetime of a single government stem directly from election promises.[19] Pressures from organised groups on Parliament or the executive often lead to decisions taken not only in the absence of electoral commitment but also in the face of hostility from substantial sectors of public opinion, such as the abolition of capital punishment. Policy can be motivated by what is considered morally right or in the public interest as well as electorally advantageous. Governments often genuinely feel they have to do unpopular things or things which have little effect on the electorate one way or the other. However it is a rare policy which is completely unrelated to some expression of group opinion.

Hence the conclusion that many political scientists arrive at from their observations of British government, 'that the policy influencing function of elections is small'.[20] Variations in governmental output can, over a long period of time, be explained by other factors. War appears to have been the great determinant of patterns of expenditure in Britain.[21] Elections may provide a legitimate method of solving the problem of political succession but they do not determine policies.

Such a conclusion, however, should not be permitted to obscure the very real problems of comparing electoral statements of intent with eventual policy decisions by the leaders of successful parties. The parties tend to make few specific promises when in opposition which can be compared with later performance in office. Criticism of the government's recent record may be a better electoral strategy than declaring commitments to specific policies. The parties may vary in this respect, however, with Labour more ready on ideological grounds to declare a programme.[22] Nevertheless the parties tend to fight elections and take office without detailed administrative plans, a factor which may, as we will see later, put their leaders when in office at the mercy of their permanent official advisers. There is also some evidence that governments perceive their electoral fortunes as dependent on the good management and solution of pressing problems. Thus what to the opposition may appear as an electioneering gambit or deviation from electoral pledges will to the government be conceived as a competent and responsible reaction to the needs of the moment and therefore quite in line with the promises made to the electorate, especially when those promises were couched in terms of 'building a better Britain', 'peace and prosperity' or vaguely defined improvements in specific aspects of life, such as health or housing.

Local elections

General elections are not the only opportunities to exercise electoral power. There are local government elections every year. District councils elect a third of their members for a four-year term of office in three years out of four. In the fourth year when there are no district elections all the members of county councils retire, also after a four-year term, and elections are held for all the seats on the councils. County councillors represent single-member divisions and district councillors represent wards which return three, or in metropolitan districts a multiple of three, members. In this way democratic, representative government is carried over into local administration.

The political parties are also active in local government and are likely to become more so under the new system introduced by the Local Government Act of 1972. Such a development should strengthen the connection between policy choices and electoral choices in the minds of voters. In the 1973 elections the national parties fought in all the local authorities in England and Wales, although some constituencies and wards may have been contested in the absence of national party candidates. Of all the county and district council seats available, the national political parties won 75 per cent, and the independent candidates and local parties won 25 per cent.

However the picture of electoral choice of local policies is as complicated as it is in national government. First, the opportunity to express policy preferences through local elections is rarely taken. Or to put it another way substantial proportions of local electorates appear satisfied with or apathetic about whatever the candidates propose. For reasons which are by no means clear local electorates are indifferent to policy options offered at election time. Although there are considerable variations within a given type of local authority, turnout at local elections on average accounts for less than 50 per cent of the electorate.

Even this of course assumes the existence of an electoral contest, for in the rural areas between two-thirds and three-quarters of council seats have in the past been uncontested. Urban areas have more elections but even in such localities between 10 and 30 per cent of the candidates may be returned unopposed.

Secondly, in local elections fought on party lines there is a marked tendency for local electoral fortunes to reflect the national popularity of the parties rather than the impact of local issues on voters' choice. If the effect of the new system of local government is to extend the local activities of the national parties then the correlation between voting trends in local and national elections is likely to be found in more and more localities. Despite variations in the needs of localities and the performance of local councils, 'the close conformity of local electoral behaviour to national political trends . . . suggests that this variety, in promise and performance alike, makes little impact on the general public'.[23] Herein lies the paradox of local government. By creating electoral situations to prevent the exercise of arbitrary power, to enforce accountability and to provide for the popular choice of leaders and policies, local government may be attracting party activity which motivates the electorate to base its judgements of the local situation on irrelevant, national considerations.

The fact still remains, however, that sometimes the election results in a particular locality do not reflect the national trend. Even here, however, they do not seem to be associated with local issues and controversies; and in one study it was found that the most controversial local issue since the war, which everybody thought would adversely affect the local fortunes of the majority party on the council, in fact left it doing slightly *better* than the party nationally.[24]

The conclusion is supported by more general survey data. Partisan preferences seem to be carried automatically from national to local politics. Involvement in local issues at election time is slight. Over 90 per cent of the respondents to the Butler and Stokes survey voted locally for the party to which they gave their support nationally.[25] The only way to interpret this as a choice of local policies is to assume (and this is not unrealistic) that the local electorate feel confident in the party of their choice and are prepared to hand over broad responsibility to it for local as well as national affairs, whatever they might be.

Thirdly, it is argued that local authorities, always dependent on Parliament, have increasingly become subservient to the central government and mere administrative agencies of central departments.

Whatever autonomy they might have in theory, enabling them to respond to popular demand and choice, in practice has been whittled away by central controls over local services. The truth of these allegations will be examined in a later chapter.

THE POLITICAL CULTURE

Whatever we may conclude about the power of individuals in electoral situations one factor cannot be denied: social values create a culture within which government is carried on. The political culture constrains government in a number of different ways. It is through the establishment of normative rules governing political behaviour that popular sovereignty is exercised. Lest it should be thought that this is to ascribe an insignificant role to the citizen, it should be pointed out that the very stability and existence of the system itself is dependent upon there being a degree of consensus that the system is working as it should.

The values which define the legitimacy of government relate to the geographical boundaries of the political community, the regime (or constitution), expectations of political roles and the performance of government.[26] If the boundaries of the community are called into question, as they are to varying degrees by the Celtic nationalists, the results may range from modifications to the machinery of government (such as the appointment of a Secretary of State for Wales) to secession, depending on the intensity of feeling. If the regime is called into question by enough people the result will be violence, *coup d'état* or revolution. Both such developments concern the viability of the system as a whole. The other two sets of values, relating to roles and governmental performance, are more relevant to the policy outputs of a system of government.

The evaluation of political roles serves two purposes. It defines who is entitled to exercise political rights; and it enables the individual to judge his own performance in politics. The former is to a large extent embodied in law and the constitution, through the Representation of the People Acts and the legal guarantees of freedom of speech and associations. Less formally, such values determine how aspirants to political office are assessed — whether a particular class background, marital status, educational experience or sex is regarded as a necessary attribute of the political leader.

How the individual regards his own role in politics is more closely related to his political power. The evidence on this is rather conflicting. The Civic Culture survey revealed a fairly high level of 'subjective competence' or belief in one's own ability to exert political influence. When asked whether they thought they could do something about a proposal to introduce a national law or local government regulation which they thought unjust or harmful 78 per cent thought they could do something about it at the local level and 62 per cent at the national.[27] Fewer thought it likely they would try, and fewer still reported having attempted to influence government. Leaving aside doubts about how far the results reported on this part of the survey adequately distinguished between the feeling that the individual could act and the feeling that such action was likely to succeed (two *very* different things), a fairly high level of civic competence seems to have been revealed.

Other surveys, however, suggest differently. Half the people interviewed by Butler and Stokes reported that the government did not pay much attention to what people think, except at elections.[28] Here 72 per cent said they thought that having elections made the government pay attention to what the people think. This is particularly interesting when compared with the Civic Culture finding that only 4 per cent mentioned voting as a strategy of influence. The majority said they would either organise informal protests or make an individual approach to elected representatives or the press.[29] The patterns of response were very similar for both national and local government. A survey carried out in Stockport in 1964 produced findings consistent with those of Butler and Stokes: 65 per cent claimed that people like themselves had little or no influence on the way the country is governed, but 60 per cent thought that the electoral process gave voters a big influence on the way the country is governed.[30]

It is difficult to know what conclusion to draw from such conflicting evidence on the citizen's perception of the significance of his or her political acts. One conclusion might be that although the citizen regards elections as collective decisions of some importance for the control of government he does not feel he can make much impact outside the electoral situation without the cooperation of others. Hence the importance of group activity in politics. What is probably more important than how people feel about their competence to act effectively in politics is whether they feel that the competence they have is enough, or whether they feel alienated. Values and attitudes on these questions are relevant to consensus and stability.

The individual's perception of legitimate political roles extends to the activities of collective groups. It has now almost become a convention of the constitution that the interests likely to be affected by developments in public policy have, through their representative associations, a right to be consulted by policy-makers. Governments are regarded as having a corresponding duty to consult before taking final decisions. The machinery of consultation grows steadily more complex so that policy-making rarely proceeds without the involvement of advisory bodies, the publication of different types of consultative documents or the appointment of Royal Commissions. The right of collectivities to be consulted is an established part of the British political culture. Now and again expressions of individualism are heard, particularly from members of less powerful groups, in the form of objections to the power of some organised interests. However there would be widespread dissatisfaction with any government which consulted sectional interests merely by reference to the nation's elected representatives in Parliament. Functional and occupational representation is at least as important in our political culture as individual representation, if not more so.

Finally there are values and beliefs about the legitimate scope of state action. There seems to be a broad consensus on the generally beneficial impact of government, on the need for gradual, rather than revolutionary, change, and on a range of issues regarded as immune from state control such as religion and artistic endeavour.[31] It is also thought that liberty is favoured more than equality. There are certainly important and powerful interests which successfully resist state intervention to equalise opportunities by interference with the freedom to accumulate wealth, purchase health and educational services and speculate with the country's economic resources. While it was thought right or natural that such inequalities should exist, consensus towards the policy-making process which permitted them was not undermined. It may be that such a consensus is breaking down under a growing egalitarianism which could have serious consequences for the stability of the British political system.

While the electoral consequences for policy-making might be slight at any given time the fact remains that public opinion generally explains certain features of the policy-making system. In the long term it is the things which people believe and the assumptions which they make which determine the scope of state power and involvement in society.

It is not enough to say that the wars of the twentieth century account more for our pattern of public expenditure than any other factor. Other states, such as the USA, have experienced war but the scope of state intervention and policy-making in them is very different from Britain. Different ideas about the legitimate scope of government action must play their part.[32] It may be that statistically policy-making, as measured by levels and types of expenditure, is correlated with demographic and socio-economic variables which push aside the claims of voters, parties and even leaders. Nevertheless there has to be some reaction to such variables. Human agents have to choose to do something about slums, poverty, pollution and disease — indeed they have to invent such words to show disapproval of certain social phenomena. Ultimately policy-making can only be explained by the ideas and opinions of people.

In the short run governments take public opinion into account in two ways. They perceive it very broadly as an indication of likely reactions: what people will not stand. This is a negative influence on policy-making. And they see it as a positive influence in terms of demands for government action, but here public opinion is likely to be group opinion with a specified leadership. In British politics informed, organised, group opinion makes demands on the government or is consulted by a government intent on forming public opinion. Government response to unorganised and probably less well-informed opinion follows later in an attempt to calculate reactions and electoral consequences. Public opinion, as distinct from the pressures of organised groups, is 'a power without independent existence; a power too elusive to be cornered, taken, and delivered up as a solid political advantage'.[33] Therefore if we want to know how influential the individual can be we must study him as the member of a group organised for political action.

THE POWER OF THE MEDIA

Before turning to pressure group power the analysis of relationships between the citizen and the policy-makers must be completed by a study of the media of communication which channel information between the two and so help shape their reactions to each other's decisions. It is assumed that a prerequisite of democracy is a 'free press'. This freedom can and should be extended to the other media of mass communication, radio and television. The mass media in a healthy democracy act as effective, two-way channels of communication between government and the governed. They communicate information to the citizen about the decisions which governments have taken. In this way the media shape public opinion and help form the reactions which the public make, through elections and other types of political activity, to government policy. At the same time the media help the public articulate their demands and communicate them in political terms. By reporting on political movements and trends in opinion and by publicising specific causes the media are one source of information for the government on the public's reactions to contemporary issues and problems. The media act as the watchdog over the government and a barometer of public opinion.

If such vital communicating roles are performed by the mass media it is important to know whether they are politically biased in their presentation of news and information. Are they simply a channel for the communication of other pressures and influences or do they constitute a political power in their own right? The media interpret as well as inform. If they are biased in the way they present the actions of governments to the public or public opinion to the government they may distort democracy. If they consistently present a favourable interpretation of one approach to politics, of one party programme or one type of political action then they are definitely detrimental to democracy. Hence the concern expressed from time to time at the concentration of newspaper ownership, at the threat of proprietorial or trade union interference with the rights of editors and at the dependence of the press on private commerce through advertising revenues; or when Labour Party alleges that the BBC's coverage of the second 1974 election cost the party votes; or the Conservative Party claims that ITV is run by left-wing radicals. The facts of the interrelationships between the media, the public and government are not easy to disentangle. An attempt must nevertheless be made, since if the media influence the public's reactions to government and the government's reactions to the public, to this extent they influence public policy. It becomes imperative to ask how influential the media are in forming the individual citizen's political demands to which the government is responsive.

One way of influencing policy-making indirectly is to influence the way people elect governments. How do the media present the parties to the electorate? In the short run the media may well have an impact on the electoral success of a political party. At a general election, for example, the media may base their coverage on the personalities of the political leaders, rather than the issues. In so doing they may favour one party at the expense of the others. Similarly they may favour a party by selecting certain issues for concentrated attention. The Liberal Party seems to have gained substantially from campaign exposure by the mass media in the last ten years. Alternatively their general approach to the campaign may affect turnout. Since differential abstention can be highly influential in determining the result of an election, this is one way in which the impact of the media may be registered.[34]

In the long term there is no doubt that the mass media perpetuate a particular ideology and that the plurality of expression represented by the media is contained within a liberal political system and a capitalist economy. Hostility to socialism and organised labour is a manifestation of the support which the media give to the *status quo*. The overwhelming bias of the media is towards conservatism or mild reform within existing economic and political values. Diversity of opinion, freedom of expression, informed criticism, toleration of dissent, political independence – all these qualities of the mass media valued by liberal ideology exist, but within a framework of values from which radical alternatives are excluded by sheer weight of orthodoxy. Whether one sees the media as 'weapons in the arsenal of class domination' is neither here nor there at the moment. What seems inescapable is that: 'Given the economic and political context in which they function, they cannot fail to be, predominantly, agencies for the dissemination of ideas and values which affirm rather than challenge existing patterns of power and privilege.'[35] It is important not to overlook this bias when considering the role of the media in forming and communicating public opinion on policy options.

In the medium term, which is the really significant time span for political activists who broadly accept the canons of liberal democracy and capitalism, the media either do not appear to be party politically biased or, if they are, make little impact on electoral choice. Since the last war newspapers with Conservative tendencies have almost always had a greater share of newspaper circulation than Labour and Liberal papers combined. But this 'dominance' has certainly not been reflected in the proportion of the vote won by the parties at general elections.[36] There is also a lack of correlation between the partisan bias of newspapers and their readers who, as the evidence from survey data

shows, select their papers for reasons other than political viewpoint. At
least a quarter of the readers of Labour and Conservative papers
support the other party.[37] Even where the partisan tendencies of
readers and their newspapers are the same the reasons for a choice of
newspaper have practically nothing to do with politics.[38] As Colin
Seymour-Ure puts it: 'Teeming shoals of votes do not lie ready to be
trawled by press magnates.'[39]

In fact the mass media generally seem to confirm rather than
determine party preferences. Alternatively they provide information
which may lead to a change in party preference being made quite
independently of what was intended by the source of the information.
In a study of television's impact on the 1959 general election Trenaman
and McQuail found a 'universal rule that the electorate was *not*
influenced directly in its voting or political attitudes, either by the
amount of the political campaign to which it was exposed, or by the
presence or absence of any part or of virtually all the campaign'.[40] As
is the case with choice of newspaper, exposure to political programmes
on television appears to be motivated by other factors than a desire for
guidance on electoral choice, such as generally keeping up with what is
going on, seeing what a party might do if it wins an election and what
its leaders are like, or enjoying the excitement of a campaign.[41] Only a
small minority of people seek help from television in deciding how to
vote. Even those who do seem to be uninfluenced by the persuasive
efforts of television programmes.[42]

The partisan loyalties of the press have declined since the war and
there is now far less unquestioning allegiance given by a newspaper to a
party. The role of the mass media as critic of the government has
undoubtedly been encouraged by the growing contribution of television
to the coverage of political events.

Political impartiality is not the sole quality which we look for in the
mass media. If the citizen is to make informed and rational decisions
about public policy the media of communication should be of a high
standard all round. There is considerable concern that the quality of the
media, in providing the public with information about government
which can be used effectively in the political system, is not as high as it
might be. It is felt that the ability of the press in particular to deal with
political issues is impeded not only by the scope and complexity of
government but by legal and political rules such as the Official Secrets
Act, Parliamentary privilege, ministerial responsibility and the laws of
libel. The secrecy of British government is often contrasted with the

openness of politics in the United States. The conventions of political conduct also reduce the quality of political reporting, such as the discretion and remoteness of politicians, the hostility of the judiciary and the 'Establishment' links between the senior editors, the proprietors and the political elite.[43]

At the local level there is also concern about the adequacy of the media as public watchdog. Press coverage of local government is declining in quality and there seems to be no strong pressure from either councillors or the public to reverse the trend. Very few councils allow the press access to even their main committees. Editors and proprietors believe that they are satisfying what little demand there is from their readers for news of local politics. It is unlikely that the local press could significantly affect political attitudes, but there might be grounds for concern that dependence on advertising revenues leads to editorial policies which emphasise entertainment at the expense of political information, communication and criticism.[44]

ORGANISED INTERESTS

Although the realisation seemed to dawn rather late on many observers of British politics, it is now widely recognised that the exercise of political influence through organised groups is a dominant feature of British government. Opinion as to the *desirability* of this state of affairs varies, but it is undisputed that for the individual to have any hope of influencing the decisions of the government which he has helped bring into being he must work through an interest or pressure group. For the ordinary individual the pressure group is a more important channel of communication and power than the political party, a fact of great significance to the overall distribution of power in British society, as will be seen below.[45]

Pressure groups are organisations with formal structures whose members share some common interest. For the most part they seek to influence the decisions of government without attempting to occupy political offices. Pressure groups may be said to articulate interests, while political parties aggregate those interests into a working majority view which can win power. Nevertheless pressure goups sometimes sponsor candidates in elections in order to test support for their cause. They are rarely, if ever, successful. Leaders of organised interests may be recruited into administrative and consultative roles, and serve on managerial boards and government advisory bodies. The distinction between pressure groups and government offices or agencies is further blurred by the fact that public bodies, such as local authorities, the universities and the nationalised industries, may from time to time engage in lobbying activities.

Many pressure groups are not exclusively concerned with political activity and influence. Some organisations which exert immense influence have other functions. The Confederation of British Industries, for example, provides a wide range of industrial and advisory services to its constituent bodies on subjects such as new legislation and regulations, prices, insurance, management problems, patents and trade marks, taxation and even town and country planning. It is important here to introduce a distinction between different types of pressure groups, since some are more likely than others to be totally concerned with political action. More important for the study of power in policy-making, some groups are thought to exercise more power than others. The distinguishing features of these types of organisation are important in the assessment of factors contributing to the power of groups.

It is usual in the study of British government to distinguish between two main kinds of pressure groups, while acknowledging that particular instances of pressure group activity may well overlap the analytical boundary. First there are sectional interest groups, such as trade unions, professional associations, the British Medical Association, the Confederation of British Industries, the motoring organisations and, in local government, tenants' associations and residents' groups. The aims of such groups are determined by the needs and interests of their members, whether they be individuals or corporate bodies grouped together in some form of confederation. Their leaders, executives and spokesmen are usually assumed to be the representatives or delegates of the membership. Sectional groups protect interests. They add a new dimension to a system of government whose scope continues to expand.[46] Functional representation is added to the individual and community representation provided by an elected legislature. Sectional groups enable occupational, economic and social interests to be represented in the process of developing public policy.

Promotional groups on the other hand seek to promote causes and are consequently more overtly political in that lobbying is their *raison d'être*. Their aims are not determined by the interests of their members who are usually not representatives of any social group likely to benefit from their policies. Promotional groups either appeal to the conscience of the public generally or to sectional interests in particular. Their cause is the public interest whether perceived in religious, educational, humanitarian or ethical terms. Where a sectional interest stands to benefit from the success of a promotional group it is usually because it is incapable of adequately defending itself. These general points about promotional groups are illustrated by a selection of examples: the Child Poverty Action Group, the Campaign for Nuclear Disarmament, the Howard League for Penal Reform, the National Society for the Prevention of Cruelty to Children, the Council for the Preservation of Rural England, the Committee for Environmental Conservation, the Royal Society for the Prevention of Accidents.

This basic distinction between sectional and promotional is useful for analytical purposes, but cases occur when sectional interests lie half-hidden behind a cause. Some of the leading members of the temperance movement were chocolate manufacturers. The National Smoke Abatement Society was supported by manufacturers of smokeless fuels. In appealing for more resources for educationally deprived areas teachers also appeal for a better financial deal for themselves.

It is impossible to predict the circumstances under which a group can expect to be successful in influencing the emergence of public policy. There are too many countervailing forces, within government itself and among competing groups. However it is possible to explain the relationship between groups and government in such a way as to reveal those aspects of policy-making which provide opportunities for the successful exertion of pressure and influence.

Dependence

A price which a government may have to pay for its intervention in some area of social or economic life is a degree of dependence on affected interests. This dependence may come about for a variety of reasons. First there is the government's dependence on the cooperation of private interests in the implementation of policy. Many governmental powers would be incapable of execution without the cooperation of vested interests. Such interests can demand a say in the formulation of policy as a price of its successful implementation. The Health Service is an outstanding example. Having decided to provide a nationally-run and government-owned Health Service there is little that can be done unless the consent of the medical professions is secured. Hence every development in health care has to be planned with these professions in order to secure their acceptance of changes which they themselves have to carry out. The same is true for many of the industrial and commercial policies of the government.

Dependence on the cooperation of private interests may be taken further and the administration of public policy actually delegated to them. At local government level organisations such as the NSPCC, WVS and the Council for the Unmarried Mother and Her Child are involved in the machinery of welfare service provision. At national level the planning and financing of higher education is largely delegated to the University Grants Committee, a body composed of university representatives. The Law Society administers legal aid and tax is collected under PAYE by employers supplied by the Inland Revenue with tax tables and code numbers.

Producer groups and sectional interests are more likely to be able to exercise influence in this way than promotional groups. So far as the latter seek to protect a section of society (such as the poor or the aged) they do not, almost by definition, represent an interest on which the government is in any way dependent. Similarly promoting a cause on moral grounds, such as the abolition of capital punishment, involves no direct sanction or withdrawal from government of the valued resource of cooperation. Thus the promotional group must seek other sanctions against the government and in particular will attempt to influence parliamentary and public opinion in order to bring about a change of policy.

Alternatively it can try to create a different kind of indispensability, namely expertise. If a group can bring knowledge to bear on a subject, especially knowledge which is not available within government itself (for example, among civil servants), it may be regarded as an authority to be consulted. Again it is easier for sectional interests to appear as convincing experts, since workers, professionals, industrialists and technologists have first-hand knowledge of the activities which governments may attempt to change by the development of new policy. If a sectional interest loses a monopoly of expertise it will have to look for alternative sources of power if it is to continue to influence policy-making. The motoring associations are an example of organisations which have lost the near-monopoly of technical expertise about motor vehicles which they once had.[47] The motor manufacturers, however, are always consulted about changes in policy affecting the things on which they have technical expertise, such as safety rules affecting the construction of vehicles.

Promotional groups are not denied access to consultations on policy, however, if they are prepared to establish a reputation for themselves as an authority in their particular area of concern. A notable example is the Howard League for Penal Reform which has established close links with the Home Office and a high reputation in official quarters for the quality of its research into penal matters. This ability to speak with an authoritative voice on policy issues is closely related to another resource which a pressure group may need to cultivate: responsibility.

Responsibility

'In modern British politics,' writes William Plowden, 'it is a sound rule-of-thumb that there is an inverse relationship between an interest's political effectiveness and the intensity of its public protests.'[48] The benefits which stem from an image of respectability are associated with the opportunities which exist for organised groups to confer with ministers and officials at the planning stage of public policy. Groups which wish to establish close working relationships with departmental officials must inevitably forego the more dramatic and direct appeals to the public which can be made by demonstration and propaganda. The situation is perfectly summed up by the words of a Home Office minister in an address to the Howard League. 'It could be said, in these days of the sit-in or sit-down, the demo and the thunderous denunciation, that the Howard League's approach to its task is unfashionable. As one who represents "the receiving end", I would like to assure the League that an institution like the Home Office does not take less notice of comments and criticisms because they are calmly and rationally expressed, and manifestly rest on a real attempt to understand the problem.'[49]

The self-discipline demanded by the norms of officialdom may be more than some radical groups are prepared to tolerate; but some of the more militant forms of lobbying have to be abandoned if contact is sought with the official planners. Because of the power of the executive in general and Whitehall in particular, most groups who do not see themselves as outside the system altogether will eventually want to try to convince the official policy-makers that they have a positive contribution to make to their work.

In the British system of government the successful groups are precisely those which have obtained access to the executive, rather than Parliament or public opinion. The executive is the main target and for the purpose of detailed negotiations this means the officials. These are the people who have to be won over: 'All-out onslaughts on the government are worse than useless if they alienate permanent officials with whom the organisations have to deal, and whose help they may sometimes need . . . The weakness of Parliament makes it all the more important to keep informal contacts with civil servants, as well as the more formal relationships through membership of departmental and other committees.'[50]

The above analysis would seem to be equally applicable to local government. Councillors and local officials react to the reliability, helpfulness and style of pressure groups in much the same way as politicians in central government. Greater sympathy is shown to groups who use 'correct' methods and the 'proper channels'.

As in central government the more radical groups are likely to be held at arm's length. The greater the conflict between the group demands and councillor perceptions of local government, the longer the arm.[51]

Another aspect of the respectability and responsibility of pressure groups in the eyes of ministers and civil servants is their representativeness. The more the leaders of an organisation are seen as genuinely representing the people they speak for, the more weight their views are likely to be given. This fact of political and administrative life can work against the promotional or cause groups, for they have no obvious constituency. Those who try to protect the interests of the mentally handicapped, the poor, the disabled or the aged usually have very different social backgrounds. However this is not true of all promotional groups. There is often a degree of self-interest reflected in the membership of groups trying to change the law on abortion, homosexuality, divorce and the treatment of offenders, for example. Unfortunately for them, this does not compensate for the fact that they are the groups which can be branded as deviant or radical. They are certainly in conflict with established moral, conventional and religious values, thus incurring the hostility of groups which stand to defend such values. The Church, the legal profession, the police, the Mothers' Union and the Society for the Protection of the Unborn Child are examples.[52] To be able to accuse the leaders of an organisation that they do not reflect the opinions and demands of their members is a useful weapon for the politician who wants to resist pressure from a particular direction;[53] and it is one which is more readily available for use against the cause than the sectional interest groups.

Access

The image which a pressure group can create of expertise, cooperation, respectability and representativeness is related to the access which the group can have to the different stages of the policy-making process. The more points on which pressure can be brought to bear, the greater will be the group's influence. If a group cannot exert influence at all stages it is vitally important that it should have access to the stage at which policy is being planned in the departments of state. Since the government dominates the legislative programme of Parliament and can usually secure the required majorities in the divisions on different stages of a bill the powerful pressure groups are those which can influence ministers and their departments at the planning stage before a bill is drafted.

Sectional groups are more likely than promotional or 'cause' groups to be in a position to influence ministers and officials before the government commits itself to legislative enactment. The ethical causes which need to be promoted by legislation are heavily dependent on the support of individual backbenchers and their success in obtaining the time and support for private members' legislation. The government is unlikely to put its weight behind proposals which are at variance with conventional morality and it is rare for there to be a party commitment to a specific moral cause. Ministers are too preoccupied with economic and technological problems to be concerned with the needs of 'deviants' — criminals, homosexuals, divorcees — or radicals presenting a fundamental challenge of established values.

The promotional group must, for the most part, concentrate on lobbying the House of Commons in the hope of finding an opportunity to promote its own legislation or to change, usually at the committee stage, the details of legislation initiated by the executive. A group may petition a minister and give evidence to an official committee or commission of inquiry in an attempt to involve the government in policy-making and so form an alliance with the legislative majorities which favour government legislation. But the main weapon must be the campaign to influence friendly MPs and perhaps significant sections of public opinion by the force of argument. In these attempts the cause group is at the mercy of parliamentary practices which severely curtail the power of the backbencher (see Chapter 5).

In addition to this the cause group can at the most hope to secure the membership of some MPs in their organisation. Sectional interests, on the other hand, are much more closely allied to the party blocks which dominate the House of Commons. Many trade unions are affiliated to the Labour Party, while business organisations are aligned with the Conservative Party. Sectional interests benefit from alliances with the party organisations to which MPs owe a loyalty which usually overrides other considerations. Promotional groups do not.

Pressure groups from both categories use the public opinion campaign from time to time in attempts to bring influence to bear indirectly on government or Parliament. A group may be constrained in this by the fact that it has chosen to adopt an air of respectability to gain frequent and perhaps informal access to ministers and senior officials. It may choose to win the confidence of policy-makers rather than the public. To do this it may have to restrain its public statements and refrain from direct action to publicise or win support for its cause. For the sectional interest, with regular and frequent contacts with government leaders, direct action is usually a last resort, as in the case of 'industrial' action by hospital doctors. For the cause group, appeals to public opinion are usually the first stage of its campaign, to be followed later perhaps by negotiations with policy-makers in government. Publicity campaigns are often directed towards organisations other than those of central government. The equal pay campaign for example was aimed at trade unions, local government and the political parties.

The most effective moment for a pressure group to act is after the government has decided to legislate but before a bill has been drafted. It is becoming increasingly common for governments to encourage this by publishing a consultative document or Green Paper setting out the government's ideas and proposals and inviting comment from interested parties.[54] Even more common is the practice of consultation in the drafting of statutory instruments. This has tended to become almost a joint responsibility of a government department and its client groups and associations. Consequently it is thought that, with some notable exceptions, administrative details are the concern of organised interests rather than major principles or policies — groups are involved in the 'politics of detail' rather than the 'politics of issues'. The strength of a government's commitment to a principle and the consequences for it of changes in the details of policy are obviously important factors in determining the power of organised interests on any particular occasion. A vague intention to make a policy change may leave all the details (and therefore all the policy) to be made during negotiations. Similarly a very specific policy might be overturned by pressure group action.

Consultations between ministers and the leaders of organised interests form a continuous process and range from the formal, statutory obligations placed on ministers to consult, as in the case of agricultural price reviews, to the appeals and deputations to ministers made outside any formal machinery. Both types of organised interest engage in the day-to-day business of being consulted or giving unsolicited advice. All forms of communication are used, from the after-dinner speech to the committee discussion.[55] The advice of the sectional group, however, is likely to be sought by the government, whereas the promotional group has to take the initiative in communicating its views to ministers.

One important medium of communication between the government and organised interests, especially sectional interests, is the advisory committee. A large number of committees, councils and commissions advise ministers on various aspects of government policy and so contribute to the processes of decision-making. There is great variation in the use of advisory bodies. One common element, however, is that the products of advisory bodies are reports and recommendations which are not binding. Ministers can accept or reject them, remaining responsible to Parliament for their decisions. Ministers can and do take decisions without reference to advisory bodies if it suits them.

Advisory bodies may be standing (for example, the National Advisory Council on Training Magistrates, the Council for Scientific Policy and the National Economic Development Council) or *ad hoc* Royal Commissions and departmental committees of inquiry.[56] Most advisory bodies are national, but some are regional (economic planning councils, for example) or local (such as the national insurance advisory committees).

The membership of advisory committees, except when they consist wholly of experts looking into a purely technical matter such as the measurement of grit and dust emissions, reflects the extent to which such bodies provide opportunities for the representation of sectional interests. Even where the subject is technical the members of the advisory body are often drawn from those with a direct interest in the subject under investigation, as in the case of the Working Party on the Hospital Pharmaceutical Service (1968–70). Some committees are wholly representative in composition. Where there is a mixture of representative and expert membership the latter is unlikely to be drawn from promotional groups.

Membership also reflects the functions which advisory bodies perform. Some are consultative and usually consist of representatives from sectional interests and members of the executive – ministers or civil servants. Others are committees of experts, such as the Central Health Services Council. A third group is administrative, where an executive or managerial task is handed over to a committee representing vested interests, such as the University Grants Committee.

There are both administrative and political reasons for the appointment of advisory bodies. Administratively they provide means by which ministers can supplement the advice and information received from their permanent officials by lay and expert opinion from outside. They enable ministers and officials to consult regularly with the sectional groups affected by developments in government policy, testing reactions and revealing the constraints under which policy developments will have to take place. Politically a government may use advisory bodies to endorse a policy by 'impartial' recommendation – Wheare's 'committee to camouflage'. Or the government may use the device to delay taking a decision. Another motive may be to capture the support of organised interests by involving them in the policy-making process. The consultative councils for some public enterprises are examples of committees to 'nobble' the opposition. Critics can be pacified by the appointment of a committee which creates the impression that something is being done when it is not, or that consultation is taking place when it is not (the old Council for Wales and Monmouth was one such consultative façade).

It is impossible to generalise about advisory bodies. As is so often the case in British government, there is no standard pattern of institutional development. Advisory bodies vary in the extent to which they are used in different areas of public policy, in the way terms of reference are drawn up for them, in their membership and in their methods of working. So far as any of them provide access for organised interests to the policy initiators it is the sectional interests which benefit. This is because most advisory bodies are set up to secure some form of cooperation from sections of society that are intimately involved in the execution of government policy.

Issues

It was suggested earlier that pressure groups were concerned with the 'politics of detail'. In any attempt to assess the power of organised interests in relation to a policy decision it is clearly important to know whether the issue being decided is one of major principle or merely the administrative details following from the adoption of some definite policy. The chances of successful pressure group influence are greater when the government has no fixed objective in view or has not decided upon its choice of policy.

This rather obvious conclusion may obscure a more complex reality. It can be argued that a strong party or government line may itself reflect the success of an organised interest allied to the party in power. For example, the unwillingness of the Conservative Government in October 1970 to discuss anything but the details of its proposed industrial relations legislation could be interpreted in one of two ways. It could be seen as a case of interest groups being restricted to the politics of detail. Or it could be seen as a major success of the business lobby in curbing trade union power. Cases like this illustrate the complexity of the policy-making system and indicate the importance of tracing relationships not just between groups and government, but also between groups and political parties, especially the parties in Parliament. This topic is taken up again the next chapter.

Governments are less likely to have adopted major policy commitments on the great moral issues – divorce, capital punishment, censorship, abortion – and it is here that the power of groups can be very great in initiating reform and influencing the course of subsequent legislation. Here the question is less one of detail *vs.* principle and more one of radical *vs.* conservative. It has already been suggested that the rules of the game are weighted in favour of the latter.

Resources

The final variable in the equation of group power is measured in terms of resources. The most significant resources in British pressure group politics are organisation (largely a reflection of income) and indispensable expertise. The Confederation of British Industries has wealth and expertise. 'With an annual budget of over one million pounds, nearly twelve thousand companies and associations as members, and a United Kingdom staff of some 440, the CBI is

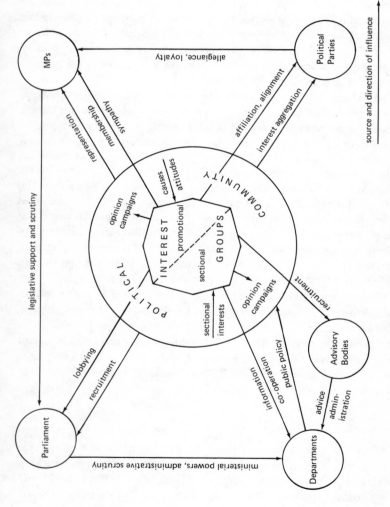

Figure 4:   Interest groups in the political system

certainly well equipped to represent the views of British Industry.'[5] [7] However its expertise and knowledge are not as indispensable as those of the BMA whose Helath Service doctors actually determine how the service will be administered to the patient. 'If doctors are powerful, it is not just because of their characteristics as a pressure group but because of their functional monopoly of expertise.'[5] [8]

These two organisations are not typical. The resources of organised interests vary greatly. The importance of indispensable knowledge has already been mentioned. If there is inequality between groups doubts may be aroused as to the desirability of group politics. It is sometimes argued that we now have something approaching a corporate state in which decisions are taken on the basis of cooperation between politicians, officials and the leaders of functional interests. Constituency representation is said to have been replaced by functional representation. The elected representatives of the people have been replaced by the leaders of sectional interests. Pressure groups now form the principal channels through which influence is brought to bear on decision-makers. Public opinion is no longer aggregated by political parties competing for office. It is differentiated and articulated by groups pursuing their separate objectives by pressuring the policy-makers.

This would be no bad thing if there were no danger that substantial sectors of society might go unorganised; or that political resources might be very unequally distributed between different sectors of society; or that the leaders of functional groups might not be representative of their mass membership. The fact that there are such dangers may lead to a rejection of the pluralist model both as a true picture of the governmental system and as a desirable form of democracy. How one judges pluralism will depend on how it is presented. The final chapter returns to this topic and investigates further the reliability of pluralism as a model of British democracy.

This chapter has been concerned with the ways in which pressure can be brought to bear on the processes of policy-making by the individual citizen using different political strategies. The complexity of the relationships involved in the exercise of power is very great, especially where the activities of organised groups are concerned. A diagrammatic representation of the web of government from the point of view of public opinion operating through organised interests is in figure 4. In the following chapter attention is focused on Parliament and the political parties as arenas for the exercise of power.

CHAPTER 5

Parties and Legislatures

The right to governmental office is conferred on the leaders of a political party by virtue of their parliamentary colleagues forming a majority in the House of Commons. Clearly the party platforms on which elections are fought constitute a basis for the party leadership when, as a government, it engages in the formulation of public policy. One determinant of government policy is thus party policy. We need to know, therefore, the distribution of power in the political parties in order to understand the forces shaping policy initiatives in government.

POWER IN PARTIES

Power in political parties is conveniently analysed from the standpoint of Robert Michels's 'iron law of oligarchy' to which reference was made in Chapter 2. In Michels's influential study of social democratic parties and trade unions the conclusion is that the organisational and psychological advantages conferred on the political and administrative leaders of even the most consciously democratic organisations create an unavoidable oligarchic relationship between leaders and rank and file. The elements of this relationship were outlined in Chapter 2. They are some help in explaining the distribution of power in British parties.

Certainly in British political parties the power of the leadership, by which is meant the parliamentary group and within that the leader himself, is very great. But it is too crude a distinction to think simply in terms of 'leadership' versus 'rank and file'. What we are faced with is a more complex set of relationships between, on the 'leadership' side of the equation, the party leaders and the parliamentary parties, the latter divided between front and backbenchers; and on the 'rank and file' side, the professionals in the party organisations and the party activists and supporters from the constituency organisations and affiliated bodies.

The really important question is the most difficult to answer: when can the influence which the different sections of a party attempt to exert over the policy-making process become decisive? In other words, under what circumstances does the leader, parliamentary party, party conference or party bureaucracy become powerful? In order to try to answer this question it is first necessary to maintain these distinctions between the centres of influence within political parties rather than see parties in terms of the simple dualism of leaders and followers. Each section of a party will have some support among the members of other sections. Conflict between the parliamentary party and the mass membership expressed, say, in terms of conference resolutions hostile to the policy of the leadership is unlikely to take the form of unified opposing groups. Rank-and-file opposition to leadership policy should for accuracy be described as opposition to a faction within the leadership group which will have its own following in the rank and file. From an analysis of resolutions to the party conferences Richard Rose concluded that far from there being a straight line-up of constituency activists versus the leadership, the rank and file was divided into the proportion which at any one time would be in opposition to the leadership, another small proportion actively in support of it, and a large proportion with no clear views on policy issues or taking no strong partisan stance: 'Factional disputes divide parties vertically, joining some Privy Councillors, MPs, lobbyists, activists and voters into a faction which is in conflict with another which also contains members drawn from all ranks of the party.'[1]

Secondly, it is necessary to distinguish between powers of initiative and powers of veto in policy-making. Not all sections of political parties are equally placed as regards the right and ability to initiate policy proposals. Those that have this right and ability have a natural advantage over those whose position allows only a response, with a possible veto if the circumstances are right, to the initiatives of others.

Thirdly, a distinction should be made between the power to initiate or veto policy proposals and a similar power over appointments to party office. The latter power is clearly only an indirect method of controlling policy and may in fact be exercised without a change in policy being an objective at all. Nevertheless the policy orientations of candidates for party office are never entirely absent from the minds of selectors and so this factor cannot be excluded from the power equation.

Indeed, if the right and ability to initiate policy changes rest predominantly with the party leadership, and the party leaders owe their positions to the rank-and-file selectors, then the latter make a real contribution to policy choice. The weakness of the selectors lies in the fact that their appointees do not regard themselves as mandated by those who choose them, do not necessarily find themselves in the majority among their colleagues in the party elite, or do not necessarily even find themselves within that elite (e.g. unsuccessful parliamentary candidates).

Under different circumstances these elements within the parties have varying degrees of influence over the outcome of policy discussions and disputes, even though the general picture which emerges is one of leadership dominance. The pattern of this dominance will be analysed by distinguishing between the two fundamental aspects of power within organisations and relating them to the structure of British political parties: the location of the right to take policy decisions; and the ability to determine who occupies the offices on which that right is conferred.

Policy decisions

The independence which the parliamentary wings of the Labour and Conservative Parties enjoy from their mass membership reflects the dominant features of the British system of government. Despite differences in organisational ideology, the internal relationships within the parties are responses to a common overriding force. On the Conservative side Tory principles of leadership actually endorse the right of the parliamentary group to be free from non-parliamentary control (although not influence). The Conservative leader is responsible for formulating policy. He or she is advised but not bound by the party's policy committees and conference resolutions. Few resolutions in fact challenge the authority of the leader. Through powers of appointment the leader controls the party organisations which can advise on policy matters. The leader can even exercise some control over entry into the group of selectors – the parliamentary party – as shown by Mrs Thatcher's March 1975 'purge' of unacceptable candidates from a party's list of approved nominees. The leader also has the right to select the members of the Cabinet when in office and the Shadow Cabinet when in opposition. Outside the parliamentary group the party has little chance to reverse a policy decision by the leader except by removing him from office. The National Union of Conservative and Unionist Associations has no power to control the leader or the party in Parliament, although it is represented on the bodies which advise the leader on policy. The leader also largely controls, through appointments, the party's Central Office. In so far as Central Office is independent of this control it is still, because of its functions and organisation, powerless to control policy-making.[2]

Labour's theory of intra-party democracy, in contrast to the Conservative Party, stresses the responsiveness of the parliamentary group to the mass membership. Yet the relationship between leaders and rank and file is similar to the Conservatives' in the formulation of party policy. The formal authority to determine policy in the Labour Party is vested jointly in the parliamentary group and the mass organisation. In theory the policies of the party are chosen by the representatives of the mass membership at the annual conference. In fact the parliamentary leaders take the initiative in the formulation of policy and have consistently refused to be mandated by the extra-parliamentary party bodies. The Parliamentary Labour Party and the National Executive Committee jointly decide which items are included in the party's programmes and manifestos. The PLP has a majority on the NEC. When the party is in office the ministerial members of the PLP are dominant in the choice of manifesto items. The NEC is usually able to win the support of conference for its policy decisions. In addition to election programmes the policies of the party are wholly the responsibility of the leadership when the party is in office. When in opposition the PLP decides on its own tactics in dealing with day-to-day parliamentary business. MPs and ministers (or ex-ministers) predominate on the policy committees of the National Executive. So far as the professional staff of the party headquarters influence policy-making, they do not do so independently but in the service of the PLP.

Within the PLP the leader exercises considerable influence over policy choices, especially when in office. In opposition the leader is in theory just the chairman and spokesman of the PLP. In practice he enjoys, as a potential prime minister, a degree of authority far in excess of any of his colleagues.

The mass membership and non-parliamentary organisations of the political parties are thus involved in a largely supporting role. At constituency level the parties are mainly concerned with raising funds, spreading propaganda, selecting candidates and fighting on their behalf in parliamentary and local elections. Social activities are also very important. Very little influence is exercised over the formulation of policy, except indirectly and tenuously by the selection of candidates. Although the central bureaucracies are more concerned with policy issues, through research activities, they do not constitute autonomous sources of policy initiative, but rather provide organisational support for the leadership. The National Union of Conservative and Unionist Associations is mainly concerned with assisting the constituency organisations and acting as a link between the party organisations and the leader. Central Office provides a professional bureaucracy to help in this work. The National Executive Com mittee of the Labour Party sim ilarly supervises and assists local and affiliated organisations through a professional organisation at head office and the submission of resolutions on Labour policy to the annual conference.

In neither party can the parliamentary leadership afford to appear dominated by party members if they are to convince the electorate that they can form a government responsive to national needs and interests regardless of party. The very nature of parliamentary democracy, in which two teams of political leaders compete for office in a continuous election campaign, means that the party rank and file mainly exist to support and serve, but not dominate, their leaders.

This theory of power in British political parties has been most forcefully presented by Robert McKenzie whose main conclusion, after an intensive study of power in the Conservative and Labour Parties, was:

> The distribution of power within British political parties is primarily a function of cabinet government and the British parliamentary system. So long as the parties accept this system of government effective decision-making authority will reside with the leadership groups thrown up by the parliamentary parties (of whom much the most important individual is the party leader) . . . Whatever the role granted in theory to the extra-parliamentary wings of the parties, in practice final authority rests in both parties with the parliamentary leaderships.[3]

The oligarchic view of political parties is strengthened by the general power within the parliamentary group of each party leader. The leader of the Conservative Party, once elected, has not in the past had to face regular re-election. The Labour Party's leader, although subject to annual re-election, in fact is rarely opposed and historically has enjoyed greater security of tenure than the Conservative leader, despite greater deference to the leader among Conservative MPs and members of the National Union of Conservative and Unionist Associations. The Conservative leader is free to choose his ministerial colleagues and appoints the senior officials of the party organisation (Central Office). The Labour leader's powers of appointment are constrained by the party constitution, but in practice there is great similarity to the Conservative leader's relationships with the rest of the party in and out of Parliament. And in both parties the fact that the leader is prime minister, or potential prime minister, gives the holder of this office great natural authority.

There is a strong tendency for conflict over policy to focus on the parliamentary leadership of the parties. For the ordinary members to have any influence on the way such conflict is resolved they must form factions by allying themselves with members of the parliamentary groups. For the great majority of members this can only be a remote and sporadic influence, exercised through indirect methods, such as mandating delegates to conferences. For the conference delegate influence is more direct but equally infrequent. For the full-time party official, the opportunities occur more frequently and the impact is potentially more direct. These activists, however, are likely to be preoccupied with other responsibilities, such as organisational and technical support to the leadership and the constituencies, and raising money.

However rank-and-file support may from time to time be crucial for the success of a faction in a conflict over policy, and this even applies to factions based on the leadership itself. In the case of the Conservative Party, once a leader is elected there is usually either consensus within the parliamentary party or conflict which is restricted to the Conservative parliamentarians. This conflict is often only resolved by the selection of a new leader. It is rare for the rank and file or party bureaucrats to play an influential role. Factionalism in the Labour Party, on the other hand, is much more common, since the party is a coalition of very different ideological viewpoints on issues of fundamental importance, such as the role of the state in the economy, defence policy and international relations. Alliances between sections of the parliamentary party and elements of the party outside Parliament have been significant on a number of occasions. Richard Rose has contrasted the Labour and Conservative Parties in terms of 'factions' and 'tendencies', concepts which refer mainly to the nature of the ideological links between MPs. However there is an organisational dimension to this contrast, which links the factions of the Labour Party to elements of the party outside Parliament while Conservative 'tendencies' are purely House of Commons phenomena. The Conservatives outside Parliament, on those rare occasions when they intervene in the power struggle between groups of MPs, do so on an individual constituency basis, disciplining members who have refused to toe the party line (as in the case of the eight Tory rebels after the Suez *débâcle*, for example). The Conservative Party outside Parliament intervenes only to enforce loyalty to the leadership. The history of the Labour Party, on the other hand, shows how policy conflicts — over Clause Four, nuclear disarmament and Britain's membership of the EEC, for example — are fought out between factions comprising sections of the Cabinet (when in office), the PLP, the National Executive and the annual conference.

Choosing leaders

The choice of policies can be influenced by controlling access to party offices. The most important offices for policy-making are leader and Member of Parliament. The general picture of the relationship between party leaders and their selectors which history provides again underlines the resilience of the former group. The party leaders themselves keep a firm grip on office, and are selected by their parliamentary colleagues, not by the parties at large. Under its most recent set of rules for choosing a leader the Conservative Party extends the right to vote to Conservative MPs who are informed but not bound by a survey of constituency opinion carried out by the chairman of the NUCA. The Labour leader is selected by a ballot of the Parliamentary Labour Party. Although formally subject to annual re-election the leader is rarely opposed. They enjoy even greater security of tenure than Conservative leaders who are particularly vulnerable if they do not bring electoral success to the party. The two parties present many important points of contrast, not least of which is the fact that while the Conservatives are prepared to delegate more policy-making responsibilities to their leader than is the Labour Party, they are less reluctant than Labour to force a leader from office if a need for a change is felt. More important still, however, is the practice in both parties of restricting power to choose the leaders to their House of Commons colleagues.

The remaining front-bench members of the parliamentary parties also enjoy stability of office. Ministers and opposition spokesmen on both sides of the House form relatively unchanging groups, their selection for front-bench status being virtually guaranteed by seniority and their seniority being guaranteed by the safeness of their constituency seats. The choice of ministers when the party is in a majority lies with the leader as Prime Minister. The choice of opposition spokesmen is also made by the leader, although in the Labour Party the choice of a front-bench team must include the members of the Parliamentary Committee elected by the PLP.[4]

It can be argued that ultimately all members of the parliamentary parties, whether on the front or back benches, owe their position to the constituency organisations which adopted them as candidates. Up to a point this power to control access to parliamentary office is a real one and is in the hands of the rank-and-file party activists. Beyond that, however, MPs have more to fear from the electorate than from the constituency organisations which select them as candidates. Once a candidate has been successful it is rare for a constituency organisation to reject him, and in the majority of cases it is more damaging politically for an MP to be in conflict with the parliamentary leadership than with his constituency.[5]

In local government it is also the case that partisan legislators (councillors) have a greater influence on policy-making in the party than the party officials or rank-and-file members. In local Labour parties the General Management Committee selects candidates to fight local elections and draws up the electoral programme. In practice the second task is usually delegated to a sub-committee on which councillors are in a majority. In between elections policy issues are decided by the councillors themselves in group meetings.[6] The same principles apply to Conservative and Liberal organisations. With all parties the degree of interaction between the councillors and the rest of the party organisation is partly dependent on the strength of the party in the local authority and the way in which partisan divisions affect the conduct of council business. The stronger the party on the council, the more likely the party group is to be subject to pressures from the party organisation on policy issues.[7]

POWER IN PARLIAMENT

The preceding part of this chapter has shown that an analysis of power within political parties must not only consider relations between elected representatives and their colleagues in the party organisation and rank and file, but must also make distinctions between different elements in the parliamentary wings. The rest of this chapter examines such distinctions in the context of conflict over the domination of legislative procedures.

Constitutional theory

In law and constitutional theory the power of Parliament is virtually unlimited. 'Within the limits of physical possibility and the limits of public opinion, Parliament can decide anything.'[8] Parliament makes the laws. The courts cannot question their validity. Indeed, court decisions can be overriden by Parliament. There is no law which Parliament could not repeal. Other bodies, such as local authorities, may only legislate with the approval of Parliament. 'Neither devolution nor delegation of legislative authority infringes the supremacy of Parliament.'[9]

In addition to its legal role Parliament has political functions of great importance. It legitimises the decisions of the government. It subjects administrative action to scrutiny and criticism. It provides a forum for the expression of complaints and grievances. The proceedings of the House of Commons constitute a continuous election campaign, in which the opposition party subjects the government to constructive partisan criticism. It authorises taxation and expenditure, and holds the government to account for its financial decisions.

In local government, too, legislative power resides in the council of elected members. Within the powers devolved to them by Parliament, local councils are the final determinants of policy. The local authority is a body corporate endowed with statutory powers and its government is the full council.

Parliamentary realities

The theory of legislative supremacy is always heavily qualified by references to the realities of parliamentary politics. The political roles mentioned above are likely to be stressed at the expense of legal formalities. It is now widely accepted that Parliament's power in policy-making is more real in a legal and constitutional sense than in terms of practical politics. The sovereignty of Parliament tells us more about the formal procedures which have to be observed in government

than about political power and influence. Hence the likelihood of
Parliament being described as a forum for 'influence, not direct power,
advice not command, criticism not obstruction, scrutiny not initiative,
and publicity not secrecy'.[10] Any control which Parliament might be
said to exercise over the executive is largely indirect, inducing
self-control and responsibility under the threat of exposure, rather than
control in the sense of determining policy and decisions, except in the
formal and legalistic sense.

This concept of parliamentary power has been formulated as a
response to the political reality of executive dominance, an historical
principle reinforced by the party system. This is not the place to
examine the debate about the 'real' nature of legislative—executive
relationships in British government. The point to note here is that the
discussion has been carried on in terms of Parliament *vs.* the executive
as if these were quite distinct and homogenous groupings.

That this is a misleading approach to the study of governmental
power is immediately evident if the analysis of party factions and
conflict is carried over from the previous section into the context of
parliamentary government. We have already seen that distinctions have
to be made even within the parliamentary leadership of political parties.
It is all the more strange that Parliament should be seen as a single unit
in competition with the executive for political power when we consider
that even apart from its bicameral structure Parliament's more
important chamber is divided into government and opposition and has
the members of the executive branch sitting in it as elected representatives and legislators.

When the effect of party is taken into account the picture is further
complicated by the distinctions which must be made, if power
relationships are to be understood, between the government ministers
and majority party backbenchers; between opposition frontbenchers or
'shadow' spokesmen and their backbenchers; and between partisan
groups of Peers. Both sets of backbenchers may be further divided into
more or less organised factions (such as the Tribune group of Labour
MPs or anti-Common Market Conservatives). Account must also be
taken of the smaller political parties, such as Liberals and Nationalists,
whose activities may be significant, especially when the government has
a small majority (or perhaps no overall majority at all). To all these
political elements which go to make up Parliament must be added the
dimension of procedural device and party organisation: the division of
the House of Commons into standing and select committees and the

division of the PLP and 1922 Committee into policy committees and groups.

Consequently the role of Parliament in policy-making is more correctly understood if Parliament as a whole is regarded as a constitutional procedural device for legitimising decisions, rather than as an independent decision-making unit. Parliament provides an accepted and orderly method for individuals and groups to exercise power. Power does not reside in (or has not been lost by) Parliament as such, but in the groups of politicians who at a particular time dominate its procedures and thereby succeed in taking authoritative decisions. It is not the strength or weakness of Parliament which is of significance to the policy-making process. Rather it is the ability of politicians to create majorities within it, whether they be Cabinet Ministers or backbenchers with varying degrees of support from outside Parliament in the parties and pressure groups.

The expression 'the power of Parliament' is really shorthand for the influence of backbenchers over ministers when a party has a large majority or of combined opposition forces over the government and its backbenchers when the majority is slim. Governments may have more to fear from their own backbenchers than from the opposition and from the viewpoint of the government benches, 'Parliament' is a rather meaningless concept. What is significant is the creation of alliances between different parliamentary groups within different procedural arrangements — the whole House for policy debates and the appropriate stages of the legislative process, for example. The functions of Parliament — legislation, granting supply, redressing grievances and scrutinising administrative action — involve procedures in the whole chambers or in committees in which alliances are formed to influence policy.

In local government power is even more diffused, with policy initiative and administrative supervision for specific groups of services being delegated to committees. Thus the executive in local government consists not of individual ministers but functional groups of councillors. The executive process is thereby something in which all councillors share, although the responsibility of none extends across the whole field of local authority policy-making.

This situation is changing under the twin pressures of efficiency and politics. The first gives rise to various planning and coordinating mechanisms such as management boards and central policy committees with varying degrees of policy-planning responsibility. Such developments inevitably draw local government towards the Westminster model by the introduction of a Cabinet system into the local council. Councillors are becoming increasingly divided into two groups, 'government' members and 'backbenchers'.

The political pressures referred to strengthen the tendency towards Cabinet government at the local level. Party influence in local politics is growing under the reorganised structure of local authorities. It is likely that majority groups will increasingly adopt the practice of filling important council posts, such as committee chairmanships and seats on policy committees, with their own members. The practice of planning policies in group caucuses is likely to spread. Under such circumstances, even if a measure of executive responsibility rests with service committees (education, highways, housing and so on), an authority's central policy committee, with responsibility for planning priorities in expenditure, formulating policy on major issues and overseeing and coordinating administrative activities, will look very much like a local Cabinet. The service committees themselves, since they are local government's equivalent of ministers, are likely to be composed of party members in proportion to the distribution of council seats between the parties (as are Parliamentary committees).[11]

The impact of parties varies. However, so far as it is correct to assume that both pressures are growing in intensity, it is probable that the analysis below of central legislative—executive relationships will become increasingly applicable to local government.

The power of the government

Nothing of what has been said so far is meant to imply that the leaders of the majority party who form the government do not stand in a powerful position in relation to other groups within the legislature. The government's power sources are well documented. They will be mentioned briefly here. Of greater importance in the present analysis are the factors which under different circumstances effectively qualify that power. But first, wherein lies the power of the government?

The most obvious source is in the support of a parliamentary majority. Governments can in most cases rely on their backbenchers to provide them with the majorities necessary to conduct government business. Despite the sanctions of Whips, and the threats of the withdrawal of party support and the dissolution of Parliament in cases of defection, support is usually given willingly. Most MPs would rather

see their party in power than the opposition, even when they disagree
with the leadership on particular policy issues. Alternatively only a
minority will know enough about or be interested in a specific issue and
so be prepared to take a stand against the government. MPs are not
lobby-fodder or sheep. The discipline which gives the parties their
cohesion is more often self-imposed than enforced on frightened and
reluctant backbenchers by the Whips.[12] Whatever its cause, however,
party cohesion is real enough and reinforces the power of the
government. The conventions of party government enable the leaders of
the majority party to control the timetable of the House of Commons and
its procedures as well as assure themselves of majority support.

Secondly, the great majority of policies sanctioned by Parliament are
initiated by the Cabinet, having been planned within the departments
of state after consultation with affected interests. Not only is most of
the legislative time of the House of Commons taken up with
government bills, but also the vast majority of them are passed into law.
The processes of consultation and planning which take place within
departments when legislation is being prepared give government proposals an authority which cannot be matched by backbench or
opposition criticism. Private Members' bills constitute a very small
proportion of the work of Parliament and then only those which
embody policies acceptable to the government are passed.[13]

Many amendments are, of course, made to government bills by
backbenchers working in standing committees. The specialisation of
such committee members may make them more prepared to defy the
Whips. However the majority of amendments of government bills passed
in standing committee are of a relatively minor and technical nature.
Successful amendments tend to be introduced by the government itself.
Thus even successful amendments which originate with the opposition
succeed because they are agreed to by the minister concerned and not
because they are forced on an unwilling government. Such concessions
are more likely to be made on less partisan policies than on legislation
which is highly ideological. In the event of concessions being forcefully
obtained by cross-party alliances in committee, they need to be
similarly supported in the House as a whole. If they are not, the
minister concerned can reinstate what was lost in committee at the
Report stage.[14]

Thirdly, a mass of legislation is made under powers delegated to
ministers by parent statutes for all the reasons familiar to students of
government: the pressure on parliamentary time, the technical quality

of much legislation, the need for time to develop proper administrative machinery, the importance of flexibility, the virtue of speed in an emergency and, not least, the political advantage to ministers of room to manoeuvre and time to plan details.[15] Only a tiny proportion of statutory instruments receive any parliamentary scrutiny at all, although what there is can be relatively effective.[16] The bulk of delegated legislation seems to be treated by backbenchers with complacent indifference.

Finally, and perhaps most important, there is a factor arising from the nature of party government itself. The party leadership, when in office, tends to move towards the centre and adopt consensus-oriented policies. Back-bench criticism is likely to come from the extremes as a consequence. This tendency is supported by the fact that back-bench opinion favourable to the opposition is likely to come under severe attack from the party outside Parliament. Therefore while a government may have to face criticism and even rebellion from its own backbenchers, it will often be able to rely on the support of the opposition which is likely to favour the government's 'moderation' rather than the 'extremism' of its critics. For example, rebellions against the Attlee administration's foreign policies were countered by Conservative support.[17] Similiarly, the rebellion of the right-wing Suez Group against Macmillan's policy on the Canal in 1957 was carried out without any risk to the government.[18] Right-wing Conservative backbenchers criticised the government's Central African policy in 1961. The government, of course, could rely on the support of the opposition.[19] Similar potential and actual coalitions in the House and in committee were in evidence on the Race Relations Bill of 1965, the Commonwealth Immigrants Bill of 1968, and the Common Market issue throughout its troubled history. Rebellion is often carried out in the knowledge that the government will not be defeated by it, often as a gesture to the party militants in the constituencies.[20] The Tribune Group's rebellion against the 'illusory' defence cuts of December 1974 was carried out only after it was clear that the Conservatives would not join them in the anti-government division lobby.

The power of backbenchers

Of course the government cannot always rely on opposition support. When it cannot the backbenchers' power becomes much more apparent.

There are six ways in which a government can find itself acceding to back-bench demands.

First, it may move away from the centre ground of politics and encounter opposition from a group of its own backbenchers large enough to form a majority in the opposition division lobby. The Conservative anti-Maplin lobby in 1973 constituted such a force. In 1974 the Labour government was defeated over the earnings rule for pensioners under the Social Security Benefits Bill by the defection of nine Labour backbenchers. In 1975 a small group of Labour MPs forced the withdrawal of the Chancellor's proposal to abolish tax reliefs for forestry by a clause in the Finance Bill.

Secondly, a government may be legislating in areas which fundamentally divide both parties, as in the case of Britain's membership of the EEC. In cases such as this backbenchers really come into their own, for the outcome is totally dependent on the coalitions which can be formed between M Ps of all parties who stand for or against a particular measure. This is nowhere better illustrated than in the parliamentary debates and divisions on Britain's membership of the EEC. The latest episode, at the time of writing, saw the Labour government with a large majority for staying in the EEC on the renegotiated terms of the 1975 White Paper but with more than half the PLP in opposition. The division in the Commons on 9 April 1975 produced the following result:

	For	Against	Abstained	Total
Con.	249	8	18	275
Lab.	137	145	33	315
Lib.	12	0	1	13
Nats.	0	13	1	14
UUU	0	6	4	10
Others	0	0	2	2

The various segments of the Labour Party in the Commons were divided as follows:

	For	Against	Abstained
Cabinet	14	7	0
Junior ministers	31	31	9
Backbenchers	92	107	24
Total	137	145	33

Conflict over policy on such issues is very likely to extend into the

Cabinet itself and further weaken the position of the executive against groups of backbenchers.

Thirdly, the opposition may have a case so reasonable that even the government is prepared to accept it. This is especially the case with details of legislation at the committee stage, when many of a minister's own amendments in fact originate from the opposition. Opposition influence can be exercised without coalitions being formed with majority party backbenchers. This is when we see the sanction of anticipated reactions at work: the government accepts proposals originating elsewhere because it does not wish to suffer the adverse political consequences of appearing unreasonable. Alternatively it may simply wish to appropriate good ideas.[21]

The opposition has three weapons with which to challenge the government. One is time. It can try to wear the government down by forcing long debates and late sittings, as the Conservatives did with the precarious Labour majority of 1950–51,[22] or by refusing to cooperate with the government's timetable.[23] A second weapon is publicity. The opposition can try to embarrass the government into changing its policy or at least force it to justify its action or inaction. The opposition 'performs a vital function in focussing public attention upon issues which Ministers might be glad to leave unemphasised'.[24] The third weapon is convention. Her Majesty's Loyal Opposition is a vital element in the constitutional system. It represents the convention that 'the power of the majority should not be used to steamroller into silence the protests of the minority'.[25] The rules of the parliamentary game prescribe that the rights of the opposition should be protected and no government wishes to risk appearing authoritarian.

It must be noted that there may be a fourth weapon which a Conservative opposition can call up. That is a natural resistance to change on the part of groups whose privileges might be threatened by Labour programmes. In other words, the Conservatives in opposition are backed by those who have something to lose, while Labour has behind it those with something to gain but whose position is consequently weaker. A Conservative opposition is likely to be strengthened by the controversies stirred up by a Labour government. The House of Lords, with its built-in Conservative majority, can be included in this type of opposition to a Labour government.[26]

A fourth limitation of the government's scope is that, although few in number, some extremely important policies are brought into operation by Private Members' legislation. One only has to think of the abolition of capital punishment, the liberalising of the laws on homosexuality, divorce, contraception, theatre censorship and abortion, and the introduction of industrial democracy to understand how such back-bench power might make 'a greater impact on the daily lives of men and women than many Government measures'.[27] The required majorities are formed by coalitions between groups which cut right across party lines and often leave the government to observe from the sidelines.

Fifthly, there is another procedure in which cross-party influence can be exerted on public policy by MPs — the select committee. These committees work in a non-partisan manner in order to assess the quality of departmental policy-making. They aim to produce authoritative critiques of policies in their designated fields.[28] A well-researched and well-argued report concerned with the efficiency, particularly in terms of value for money, with which policy objectives are achieved can make some impact on governmental decisions, if only by 'an intangible effect on official thinking'.[29] In this respect alone the relatively new Expenditure Committee should repay detailed scrutiny.

Finally, there is a sixth factor continually at work which, if only slightly more tangible in its effects, is probably the most important constraint on a government. This is the need to maintain the support and morale of the majority party. Even when a government is faced with rebellion from its backbenchers which it knows can be neutralised by opposition support, it also knows it cannot alienate the affection of its own supporters on too many occasions. Constant attention is paid, through the Whips and party committees, by frontbenchers to back-bench opinion. Excessive conflict can be damaging to the leadership's image with both the public and the party outside. It has to be resolved, but by compromise on *both* sides rather than by confrontation, expulsion or the threat of dissolution. The need for the peaceful resolution of conflict is all the more evident when it is realised that the dividing line hardly ever runs cleanly between front and backbenchers but wavers to give practically all factions and tendencies within the parliamentary parties representation in the Cabinet itself. All these points are perhaps nowhere better illustrated than in the case of the 1966—9 Labour administration's policy on industrial relations. The knowledge that the government could have forced its bill through Parliament with the support of the Conservatives was a cure more awful than the disease of factionalism which split the Cabinet and the NEC as well as the PLP, and which threatened to alienate the trade unions and destroy the party. Had Labour backbenchers supported the Cabinet, external opposition could have been resisted. But 'it was shown in 1969 that there was a limit to the sacrifices of interest and principle that the majority of Labour backbenchers would accept at the demand of their leaders.'[30] 'It was, therefore, chiefly the Government's accountability to its parliamentary majority that led to what may variably be called its compromise or surrender.'[31]

CONCLUSION

This chapter has analysed the great, though qualified, power of the government as the leadership of the majority party, both within and between the main political parties. The government of the day, however, has to contend with more than the relative power of backbenchers on both sides of the House and its own supporting party organisation outside Parliament. In addition to the group politics discussed in Chapter 4, there is the administration itself in the form of large organisations of permanent, paid officials. The next chapter looks at these extra-Parliamentary constraints on the members of the government, both individually and collectively, and includes the judiciary as an element in the policy-making process.

CHAPTER 6

Power within the Executive

Power is in part a function of authority. Authority may be conferred by office. The office-holder has the right to take decisions and expect them to be obeyed. In government such office-holders are the immediate or 'proximate' policy-makers.[1] In British government the office-holders who are closest to the points at which policy decisions are made are the members of the Cabinet. It has even been argued that an analysis of Cabinet decision-making 'would reveal the process by which decisions were made and power exercised in this country.'[2]

The first source of Cabinet power, then, is the rights conferred upon its members by the constitution. It is the constitutional task of the Cabinet to decide the policies which are to be submitted to Parliament. 'The Cabinet is the core of the British constitutional system. It is the supreme directing authority.'[3]

The second source of Cabinet power is unity. It is a rule that once a Cabinet decision has been taken, ministers must be prepared to defend it or resign. There are some notable exceptions to this rule of collective responsibility, as in the case of the 1975 EEC referendum. The convention of collective responsibility, however, usually enables the Cabinet to expect its decisions to be implemented as well as supported publicly by individual ministers. It also gains the psychological advantage of unity: 'It is essential for a strong government to show a united front in face of criticism.'[4]

Thirdly, the Cabinet is able to control and coordinate the work of the executive, through the Cabinet Office: 'Each minister, whether or not in the Cabinet, now receives the Cabinet Conclusions and it is his responsibility to instruct his department as to the decisions taken, in so far as they need departmental action.'[5] The Cabinet Office also assists the Cabinet in its other function of policy determination.

Finally, the modern party system enhances the power of executive leadership which can control a parliamentary majority by calling on party unity and loyalty. Whether one regards party unity as a function of discipline and the exercise of the Whip, or of adherence to a common cause and a unifying desire to maintain the 'right' group of leaders in office, majoritarian government under the strong two-party system ensures that the policies presented to Parliament by the executive can expect legislative support.

POWER WITHIN THE CABINET

There has been a great deal of debate in recent years, continuing with the publication of some extracts from the late Richard Crossman's diaries, about the relative power within the Cabinet of the Prime Minister. There is little disagreement over the proposition that there is a ranking and pecking-order within the government generally and the Cabinet in particular. Some ministers are more senior than others. Some ministers are politically weaker than others — in conflicts over expenditure cuts, for example. What is disputed, however, is that the power of the Prime Minister has increased in recent decmdes to the point of him being far from *primus inter pares* and becoming almost a presidential figure or 'elected monarch'.[6]

Some of this argument centres on the issue of the factors contributing to the present power of the Prime Minister. The rest of it is concerned with whether this power represents something significantly different from past political experience, whether there has been a shift in the balance of power over time. The latter issue is of less importance to the study of policy-making than the former, although it is worth recording that the historical evidence can hardly be said to prove the demise of Cabinet ministers *vis-à-vis* their chairman.[7] However it is one thing to challenge the existence of an historical trend. It is another to establish the power of the Prime Minister in relation to his colleagues under modern conditions. It is extremely difficult to know how much weight should be be assigned to the different factors which enhance and constrain the power of the Prime Minister. It is even more difficult to relate these factors to the final outcome of Cabinet decision-making in terms of policy choices. Obviously each set of circumstances surrounding a particular policy will be unique, although each will have many common elements. As a first step it is necessary to identify the general features of the power relationship which will need to be assessed when any particular policy is analysed. Whether such a feature is significant in terms of power will depend on the particular circumstances of the case. The Prime Minister has a number of 'powers'. Their importance is relative to any particular policy area.

First, the Prime Minister is said to obtain power from the nature of contemporary elections. In so far as these have become contests between party leaders, individual MPs depend for their electoral success on the popularity of their leaders. A Prime Minister can therefore expect MPs, as backbenchers or members of the government to regard themselves as mandated to support their leader.[8] Having acquired through convention the prerogative powers of the monarch, the Prime Minister can threaten dissident backbenchers with the dissolution of Parliament. MPs will step into line rather than face the prospect of a general election at which they may lose their seats.

This is a rather extreme view of the relationship between a Prime Minister and his colleagues in the parliamentary party. It ignores the extent to which electoral choice is based on images of party and the record of the previous government. However so far as a leader has some responsibility for formulating party policy, his hand is strengthened by the knowledge that MPs recognise their debt in electoral terms to the party and also generally wish to see it strong and secure in office.

The timing of a dissolution is a weapon against the opposition rather than the government's own backbenchers. For dissolution to be a threat to government MPs they would have to be electorally vulnerable. And if they are, so is the Prime Minister. But apart from this, the majority of MPs come from safe seats. It is also rare for constituency parties to penalise rebellious MPs,[9] so another election is unlikely to mean that the holder of a parliamentary seat will fail to secure his party's candidature.

Secondly, there is a whole range of debatable points connected with the Prime Minister's control of Cabinet decision-making. It is pointed out that there are areas of policy-making in which the Prime Minister takes a personal interest and responsibility, namely foreign affairs, defence and economic affairs. Certainly it is common for the Prime Minister to take a lead in these policy areas, especially in any emergency. But the Cabinet as a whole has to be persuaded of the rightness of most decisions and therefore has opportunity to modify those decisions.[10] Also there are other areas of policy, especially domestic, where the Prime Minister rarely takes the initiative simply because he does not have expertise or experience. His views will be respected because of his position. He may be of crucial significance if opinions in Cabinet are evenly divided on an issue. 'But, helpful though he may be, the Prime Minister can only defy a Cabinet majority at his own peril and by putting the fate of his government in the balance . . . There is nothing unusual about a Prime Minister in the course of Cabinet discussions being forced to modify his views, compromise, or keep his mouth shut.'[11]

It is therefore an exaggeration to say that Cabinet decisions are taken by the PM together with the responsible minister so that the Prime Minister is 'in' on all important decisions.[12] The scope and complexity of modern government make this impossible. The proliferation of Cabinet committees strengthens the position of individual ministers as much as if not more than that of the Prime Minister by increasing the supply of information and opportunities for participation in decision-making.

It has also been argued that the Prime Minister can exert exceptional influence over policy decisions through his power to control Cabinet procedure. By deciding what should be on the agenda, and by interpreting the sense of the meeting, the Prime Minister can obstruct ideas and decisions of which he disapproves. He is assisted in this by the Cabinet Secretariat which prepares the agenda for Cabinet meetings, takes minutes, circulates decisions and follows them up to see that action has been taken in the departments. It also briefs the Prime Minister personally.

While no one doubts the advantage which chairmanship of the Cabinet bestows, it is now widely agreed that a Prime Minister has to obtain the support of the Cabinet for his decisions and cannot obstruct discussions of matters which ministers wish to bring before the Cabinet. 'To carry on as leader, the Prime Minister must retain the confidence of his Cabinet, which means that he cannot dictate to it.'[13] Prime Ministers can be overruled by their Cabinets and even driven from office. Patrick Gordon Walker, who served in the Cabinet under Attlee and Wilson, concluded that: 'The Cabinet remained the sole source of political authority . . . A Prime Minister who habitually ignored the Cabinet, who behaved as if Prime Ministerial government were a reality — such a Prime Minister could rapidly come to grief . . . The Prime Minister can exercise his greatly enhanced powers only if he carries his Cabinet with him.'[14] Nor is it correct to regard the Cabinet Secretariat as the equivalent of a Prime Minister's department. It serves the Cabinet as a whole and does not match the advice and support which ministers get from their departments.[15]

Thirdly, there is the power of patronage enjoyed by Prime Ministers.

The right to nominate persons for ministerial appointment by the Queen is today a power of appointment. He can also remove ministers from office and reshuffle his Cabinet and government posts among chosen members of the government and backbenchers. As political head of the Civil Service the Prime Minister controls the machinery of government and appointments to the most senior administrative posts in the departments, particularly Permanent Secretaryships.

The power is sometimes said to enable Prime Ministers to dominate their Cabinets. They control the political futures of their colleagues. Shadow spokesmen moving into Cabinet posts after a general election will have received their shadow positions from their leader, now Prime Minister. They cannot even demand appointment to the ministerial responsibilities which they 'shadowed' in opposition: 'They can be chopped and changed at will by the Prime Minister.'[16] The Prime Minister can ensure that the senior posts in the Cabinet contain a majority of people known to be his personal supporters. Few ministers resign in protest against policies they dislike because to do so would injure the reputation of the government as well as their own political careers. Prime Ministers can usually rely on extensive support from Cabinet colleagues. When ministers do resign the security of the Prime Minister is rarely threatened, resignations being more often a result of failure to convince the Cabinet as a whole of a point of view rather than just the Prime Minister. Through Civil Service patronage the Prime Minister can dominate the crucial offices in Whitehall.

The dependence of members of the Cabinet on the Prime Minister means, it is sometimes argued, that he must be regarded as much more than first among equals. No other member of the party leadership shares his power and status, or commands anything like a comparable power base in the party. Dissident ministers, far from being potential claimants to the Premiership and therefore a threat to the security of the Prime Minister, usually spark off demonstrations of party loyalty which strengthen the Prime Minister's position against that of a possible rival. Contenders for the leadership also have far fewer opportunities to win a personal following through the mass media.

In contrast to the constant reshuffling of Cabinet posts the Prime Minister can engage in, the Premier's position is one of great security. He can be overthrown by a Cabinet *coup* or a back-bench meeting of the party. 'Both are so unlikely as to be almost impossible . . . No Prime Minister has been rejected or edged out while in office under normal conditions of party conflict in peace time in this century.'[17]

The power stemming from patronage and security should not, however, be exaggerated. Political status, experience and ability win office just as much as personal support for the Premier: 'There is little evidence to suggest that men of real ability, well qualified for office in every respect, are being kept out on account of the purely personal disfavour of the Prime Minister.'[18] Some at least of the balance of opinion in the party has to be reflected in Cabinet. Rebellious characters are not automatically denied office. Dismissals are only easy when there is a consensus in Cabinet that a minister is doing a job badly. It is much more dangerous for a Prime Minister to dismiss someone who enjoys considerable support within the party and Cabinet simply because he or she opposed the Premier. The possibility of resignation and therefore damage to the credibility of the government acts as a constraint on a Prime Minister in deciding how to handle different issues.

Civil Service appointments are made on the advice of the head of the Civil Service. 'The real discretionary power exercised by the Prime Minister over these appointments is not much greater than that of the Queen when she is presented with a list of ministers for approval.'[19]

Finally, the different personalities and styles of Prime Ministers and their Cabinet colleagues should not be overlooked. Members of the Cabinet bring different experiences and abilities to bear on the tasks of government. The type of decision-making group which this social mixing leads to varies from one Cabinet to another, making it difficult to generalise about the power of a Prime Minister. So far as power is in part a function of personality, Prime Ministerial power is not a constant factor. It varies 'according to the strength, style and aptitudes of the individual Prime Minister, and the ability, experience and determination of his colleagues'.[20] Some Prime Ministers are surrounded by experienced, able and powerful men and women. Some are not.

It is difficult to arrive at firm conclusions about power within the Cabinet. The most convincing evidence of Prime Ministerial domination concerns his ability to manipulate offices and decide on the deployment of the available political talent. The power of the Prime Minister is most evident when he is defending his own position as leader and determining the fate of his parliamentary colleagues. It is a power relevant to the scope and content of governmental offices and to the security of their incumbents. Public opinion, the electoral system and party loyalty protect the Premier against rivals and strengthen his control of appointments and promotions within the government.

But this is a power to determine who will decide, not what they will decide. It is a power related to the filling of ministerial offices rather than the formulation of policies within departments. The Prime Minister's resources for political manipulation are not matched by his resources for policy analysis and advice. The evidence of Prime Ministerial power in the development of government policy is not particularly striking. The Prime Minister may take the initiative in dealing with emergencies and major issues of foreign affairs. There may be Prime Ministerial involvement in the formulation of broad economic policies and in the management of the economy, upon which the remainder of government depends. Consequently this role should not be underestimated. Detailed policy-planning, however, is carried out in departments which support ministers with an organisational capacity that the Prime Minister totally lacks. There is no Prime Minister's department. Attempts to provide Prime Ministers in the past with policy advisers have always been blocked by departmental officials and individual ministers. The Cabinet Office serves the Cabinet collectively and anyway has never had an analytical capability. The CPRS is also committed to improving the decision-making quality of ministers collectively. More important, so far as it is able to look at a limited range of issues that cut across departmental boundaries and so provide the Prime Minister *and the rest of the Cabinet* with strategic advice, it is regarded as a threat to the departments of state and is dependent on them for information. Even if the problems of devising an overall strategy for the government are ignored, it is still impossible to see the CPRS as providing the Prime Minister with policy analysis comparable to that which goes on within a minister's own department. In cases of conflict between the CPRS and departmental advice, the departments and their ministers prevail most of the time.[21]

It may be that the real business of collective decision-making in central government takes place in Cabinet committees rather than the full Cabinet, and that many tactical and strategic decisions affecting the deployment of public expenditure or the management of the economy are finally settled by the responsible ministers in consultation with the Prime Minister. But this is a far cry from assigning dominant power to the Prime Minister in even the major decisions of government. The Prime Minister's job is to 'seek to reconcile collective rule with the individual responsibility of ministers to Parliament'.[22] He is a 'court of last resort' for appeals from the spending ministers. Once the Prime Minister's support for a policy has been obtained it will be decisive. But this is not to say that the Prime Minister need have played any part in initiating that policy. Even Richard Crossman complained of the Labour Cabinet of 1964—6 that: 'Policy is now formulated in the various Departments and merely co-ordinated by Harold at the last moment. There is no inner Cabinet with a coherent policy.'[23] Initiatives are not taken in 10 Downing Street. Cabinet ministers do not accept that the Prime Minister has an automatic right to veto proposals of which he disapproves. The crucial staff who control public expenditure and negotiate with the spending departments are not the Prime Minister's staff. Members of the government are not expendable, and need each other more than they need the Prime Minister. 'At heart, British Cabinet government retains, with a devilish twist or two, all the characteristics of government by committee.'[24]

CONSTRAINTS ON CABINET POWER

When considering the power of the Cabinet it is important to see it in two contexts, both of which impose constraints on its role of finally determining the policies to be submitted to Parliament. The conditions under which the Cabinet can command a majority in the House of Commons, thus ensuring that the policies submitted become law, were discussed in the previous chapter. The first set of constraints to be noted here stem from the political environment surrounding the whole executive branch of government.[25] There are international obligations which have to be recognised in both the defence and economic spheres — NATO and the EEC for example. There are constraints imposed by aspects of our own economy, particularly our balance of payments problems and rate of inflation. There are also crises which impose constraints on ministerial policy initiatives, such as Rhodesia's unilateral declaration of independence in 1965 and the Northern Ireland situation. Finally, as a government comes to the end of its term of office and an election looms large, it may find cooperation from interest groups and industry waning, and controversial measures becoming more difficult to implement.[26]

The second set of constraints comes from within the executive. It is unconventional to talk of the 'executive' in Britain because it is common for a rigid distinction to be maintained between the politicians in the government and the paid officials in the Civil Service. Executive work is also carried out by a disparate group of local authorities, public corporations and *ad hoc* administrative bodies which do not constitute a homogeneous executive branch of government. Nevertheless it is important, when considering the power of political leadership in both central and local government, to include the role of paid officials in the analysis.

THE POWER OF OFFICIALS

According to democratic principles government should be political, not administrative. A democracy is government by politicians chosen by the people. Government by paid officials is bureaucracy. Public servants, whether civil servants or local government officers, are recruited in theory to serve political leaders by carrying out their decisions. Ministers and councillors decide on policies and their paid officials take the necessary executive actions to implement them.

The reason why it is necessary to underline that this is the theory of political-administrative relationships is that in reality the paid official exercises much more power in the formulation of public policies than the formal description of his responsibilities suggests. The importance of the senior official's role in policy-making arises because he is concerned with ends and not merely means. It is no longer realistic to look upon senior civil servants and local government officers as exclusively concerned with the implementation of decisions made by politicians. The administrative official must be recognised as having a political, though not necessarily partisan role in policy-making.[27] There are many reasons why this should be so.

The administrative role

First, the paid official has a constitutional duty to advise on policy choices. Higher civil servants, for example, take or advise ministers to take decisions that arise within the framework of existing policy but which cannot be dealt with by routine management. This is the individual case-work which arises from legislation. An example is the decision following an appeal against a local planning authority's ruling made under the town and country planning laws. Such decisions expand or clarify the scope of a policy and finalise its application in new and special circumstances. Civil servants are further involved in this type of decision-making when preparing explanatory material for ministerial use on the operation of current policy, when answering parliamentary questions and MPs' correspondence, and when generally aiding the minister to account for the operations of his department when public attention is directed towards the effects of final decisions.

It is important to distinguish case-work from the other sense in which civil servants are required to advise on the development of policy. Here the official is concerned with the planning of new policies and with advising ministers on alternative policy options. The preparation of legislation may constitute a later stage of this activity, preceded by negotiations with outside interests.

On relatively rare occasions civil servants may be able to take full responsibility for a new measure, where a policy is outside the arena of party conflict and quite separate from other major policies. Sir Edward Playfair has described how, as an under-secretary at the Treasury, he decided that the constitutions of the National and Tate Galleries needed bringing up to date. He cleared his own proposals with the Chancellor, carried out the necessary negotiations with the trustees and other bodies and drafted the required bill. There was no political opposition to the measure and the reform was carried through.

This is a relatively unimportant expression of civil service 'power' and the conditions which made such independence of action possible rarely occur. More important is the work of the Civil Service on the development of major policies in line with government commitments. The civil servant's responsibility is to advise on the financial and administrative implications of different policy options, thus aiding ministers to find ways of achieving their political objectives.[28] The same terms could be used to describe one of the relationships between senior local government officers and council committees.

Feedback

Secondly, policy-implementation feeds back into policy-formation so that the administrator can advise authoritatively from experience on the practicability of different policy options. A great deal of legislation builds on past administrative practice and accumulated experience. The details of much new policy are conditioned by what is administratively and politically possible. The contacts which have developed between civil servants and organised interests provide information on the need for reforms. In this sense 'much of the legislation which the Cabinet is willing to sponsor comes from the permanent staffs of the Departments'.[29]

Some new policies emerge as past policies are reviewed, as in the case of the investment programmes of the nationalised industries. Other policy developments, such as the creation of new forms of transport authority under the 1968 Transport Act, may, by their very nature, present less in the way of past experience as guidance. But even in cases such as this the past acts as a restraint: in this particular instance the existing pattern of local government influenced the form which the public transport authorities took, in terms of their management and financial structures, their geographical boundaries and their relationships with other public authorities involved in transport and communications.

Expertise

The knowledge of public policy derived from direct experience of its operation gives the senior administrator a near monopoly of knowledge relevant to policy-formation. New policy emerges as administrators bring their ideas to bear on problems which political leaders wish to solve. As repositories of knowledge and experience senior officials are able to argue from positions of great strength about the administrative difficulties raised by policy proposals, the political repercussions likely to be encountered from the interests most affected, and new methods of dealing with problems for which no satisfactory solution has been found. If a minister has no strong political commitment in, say, the form of a party manifesto on a matter of even considerable public concern, then the opportunity to take the initiative in developing policy in a field in which the government is already involved, such as new towns or regional planning, if not in producing new departures in government intervention, is a very real one for a civil servant. In central government the civil servant's specialised knowledge of his policy area is certainly not matched by that of his minister.

The political backgrounds of ministers do not train them in policy analysis. The Houses of Parliament provide training in verbal, negotiating and debating skills, and constituency 'welfare'. They do not lead naturally to departmental work. There is little parliamentary training in the specific functions of government and even if there were, skill in administration is not usually regarded as a qualification for ministerial office.[30] Officials have to spend a great deal of time learning how their minister will use his own particular knowledge and experience in running the department to which he has been assigned 'out of the blue'.[31]

Most ministers do not even have the 'various knowledge' and 'miscellaneous experience' which Bagehot thought would enable the intelligent laymen at the head of a government department to oppose 'bureaucratic sense' with common sense.[32] They are professional parliamentary politicians as much as intelligent laymen, not having outside careers. Furthermore a substantial proportion of ministers apparently believe that 'the attributes of the intelligent layman and Parliamentary politician are no longer ideal qualifications for holding office'. They now believe that 'executive ability, or knowledge of specific subjects, or both, are now relevant'.[33] If ministers are not competent to plan policies, their departments certainly are.[34]

In local government there is an even starker contrast between the lay politicians and the expert officials who for the most part are professionals. The senior officials in local authority departments, responsible for policy development and implementation, have professional qualifications in subjects directly related to local authority administration, such as accounting, education, social work, engineering, town planning and public health. Even the managerial expertise increasingly being imported into local government to promote corporate planning tends to be provided by professional managers. Against this professionalism the local councillors must pit their wits, common sense and varied experience of full-time occupations in business, industry and the professions.

Another facet of the imbalance between politicians and administrators is the lack of opportunities to prepare for office when in opposition. The official opposition in central government has no access to the departments. What research facilities there are in the party organisations are often preoccupied with short term business. A Labour minister who has headed the Transport House Research Department complained in 1966 that: 'Ministers may bring with them broad ideas of how future policy should develop. But in the transformation of policy goals into realistic plans, in the execution of those plans and, still more, in policy responses to new and unexpected developments, Ministers are largely, if not wholly, dependent on their official advisers.'[35] Policies which are worked out in detail prior to winning office often prove administratively impracticable. It is impossible to anticipate all the problems likely to be encountered in office.[36]

The Labour Party's organisation for policy-planning is weaker than that of the Conservatives' which has been developed considerably since 1964. Whether the Conservative Party's record in office from 1970–74 and as an effective opposition since then can be said to have been improved by the fairly elaborate network of Conservative policy research units is probably impossible to decide.[37] Both parties in office have found it necessary to appoint numerous special advisers and advisory committees to provide them with a counterweight to Civil Service expertise and to question departmental attitudes and philosophies.[38] But neither Royal Commissions, departmental committees of inquiry nor the Whitehall 'irregulars' are entirely free from the influence of the departments to which they are attached or owe their origins.

Thus even those ministers who see their main role as that of policy initiator 'come to office without well defined policy objectives and priorities'.[39] Those who do have such objectives only have them in the most general terms: 'The majority of Ministers do not come to office with policy objectives sufficiently well defined to give their civil servants useful guidance in drafting legislation and devising administratively practical programmes.'[40] They have little choice but to rely solely on civil servants for the definition of objectives and the submission of policy proposals. Since officials are the first to handle policy problems in any detail and since there are few alternative sources of advice, ministers find it difficult to do anything other than accept or reject the advice given *in toto*. The minister can sanction or veto. He cannot plan.

Permanence

The natural authority of the senior administrators is strengthened by their permanence in office compared with the mobility required by the politician's career, especially in central government. Departmental attitudes and philosophies emerge, and while they change over time as new cohorts of administrators move up through the organisation, at any given time they are much more firmly entrenched than any minister or council committee. Richard Crossman has recorded how difficult it is to prevent ideas being reinterpreted to suit departmental attitudes: 'This eternal process goes on. Just as the Cabinet Secretariat constantly transforms the actual proceedings of Cabinet into the form of the Cabinet minutes (i.e. it substitutes what we should have said if we had done as they wished for what we actually did say), so here in my Department the civil servants are always putting in what they think I should have said and not what I actually decided.'[41] Interdepartmental contacts at official level usually precede and often predetermine interministerial contacts, i.e. the Cabinet.[42]

The frequent rotation of ministers means that the average time spent with a department is less than the average time required for a policy to be planned, implemented and assessed. The system 'does not enable the political entity anywhere to see objectives through, since the Cabinet and Prime Minister — which exist together more continuously than any individual Minister — do not scan and control the formation of objectives'.[43]

Organisational size and complexity

The scope of departmental responsibilities and the consequent size of organisation is often so great as inevitably to strengthen the influence of the permanent officials. Even in a relatively small department, such as Education and Science, a minister can only select a small number of issues for attention. Most of a department's activities continue without ministerial involvement.[44]

Ministers are remote from most levels in the departmental hierarchy, especially in the 'giant' departments such as Defence and Environment. The official attitude is that a department should be small enough for a minister to be able to handle its Cabinet business, not small enough for the minister to control his or her civil servants.[45] The minister is vastly outnumbered by his officials as is the local councillor, especially in the new, larger local authorities. In the new system fewer, smaller committees face fewer, larger departments. The number of elected representatives has been reduced by the 1972 reforms but the number of officials has greatly increased. The amount of delegation from politicians to officials is much greater than it was fifty years ago. It is not bureaucratic manipulation that has brought this about (although civil servants can be very irritated when ministers intervene in areas which they think should be left to them).[46] It is a function of the range of government business and the number of decisions that have to be taken. When ministers average about four per department it is inevitable that the senior officials, who outnumber them by about fifty to one, have to decide what shall be referred to them.[47]

This feature of modern government means that a minister's policy-making responsibilities are outnumbered by other tasks. He spends a good deal of time defending what the department has done, and quickly becomes identified with its existing activities rather than with new initiatives.[48] Ministers have to cope with larger departments, more complex and technical issues, longer parliamentary sessions and more Cabinet and committee meetings than forty years ago. The tasks to be performed in the average working week squeeze out considerations of public policy. Despite the fact that the majority of ministers regard policy initiation and selection as their most important activity and regret not being able to spend more time at it, policy matters often appear to be dealt with in whatever time is left over from other commitments.[49]

Despite this not all political executives regard policy-making as the be-all and end-all of a political career. In local government, for example, councillors have a wide diversity of aims and interests. They may concentrate on constituency or 'welfare' problems. They may see it as their role to manage the local authority or simply limit its spending. Others have a vague desire to serve the community. Other categories of roles can be identified. Not all wish to take part in broad policy decisions.[50]

In central government, too, there are many tasks which ministers are required to perform for their departments in addition to policy-selection and initiation. There is a large number of politically sensitive yet trivial decisions which require ministerial endorsement. The interests of the department have to be defended in Cabinet (for example, fighting for parliamentary time for legislation), in the House and in private discussions with MPs. The department itself has to be managed in the sense of supervising departmental organisation, maintaining staff morale, and controlling and evaluating the implementation of policies. Diplomatic functions have to be performed in consulting and negotiating with client and interest groups. The department and its policies have to be 'sold' to the political environment.

When ministers become involved in policy decisions they may even then only be able to make choices between the options presented to them by their officials. Only a minority of ministers regard the initiation of new policy as of prime importance and these appear to accept that this role is likely to make them unpopular with their senior staff.[51] Also it is probably the role for which, as we have seen, their non-ministerial backgrounds prepared them least.

The variety of ministerial roles, and their equivalents in local government, should not necessarily be regarded as unfortunate in their effects on policy formulation. Indeed politicians believe that there is a need in government for different types of minister. Jeremy Bray, for example, distinguishes between the different valuable contributions made by the 'politician', moving with public opinion; the 'philosopher', offering new concepts and values; the 'executive', trying to run a department as he would a business by defining objectives, devising programmes for attaining them and reviewing performance; and the 'representative', ensuring that the political group from which he comes is influential.[52]

These then are the factors which set the policy forming work of ministers in perspective and which must be evaluated in any analysis of the way a particular public policy was formed. But there is the other side of the coin. Just as the power of ministers is relative, so is the power of officials. The environment in which they work must also be considered.

Departmental routine

If ministers have many different roles to perform, civil servants have to support them. Officials are often too hard-pressed by day-to-day workloads and cases to be able to reflect adequately on new policy. Senior civil servants are never fully occupied with policy-planning. The administration of existing policies generally occupies the greater proportion of the time of senior administrators in government departments. Forecasting expenditure, exercising financial control, preparing explanatory briefs on current policy (for ministerial speeches, answers to parliamentary questions and so on), negotiating with pressure groups, casework and the management of subordinate personnel has led to the neglect of the policy-making function. The Fulton Committee, for example, concluded that long term policy planning was the responsibility of officials 'over-burdened with more immediate demands arising from the parliamentary and public responsibilities of Ministers'.[53]

Lest this should create a picture of senior officials desperately searching for time to impose reforms and innovations on unresisting ministers, it must be recognised that change often runs contrary to the interests of members of large organisations. Their interests lie in developing procedures of decision-making which avoid complications and conflict. Indeed they are judged by their superiors on 'their ability to do a series of practical tasks, such as drafting reports on which committee members can agree, chairing difficult meetings, and above all else in getting documents "cleared" quickly with all the many interested parties'.[54] They are rarely assessed on their policy ideas.

Personalities

Not all politicians are by any means the captives of their senior officials in policy-making. Personalities, ideologies and circumstances vary. They can coalesce to enable a minister to initiate radical change. If a minister has a strong ideological commitment to a policy, perhaps supported by a party commitment, the administrator's influence will be reduced. The minister who is prepared to delegate to his junior minister so he can concentrate on a discreet key issue, who has been able to define his objectives immediately after taking up office, who has political 'weight' and backing, and who has intellectual ability will be very favourably placed to initiate new policies.[55]

Similarly in local government the power of councillors depends on ideological commitments, the party organisation of the council and the nature of the policy — whether, for example, an official has statutory responsibilities independent of the council, or the policy area is one which attracts partisan commitments. If local councillors regard their authorities as administrative agencies of the central government, or try to take local issues 'out of politics' they correspondingly increase the power of the official. Decisions will be regarded as technical matters requiring professional interpretations of central directives or local needs.

Competition

Finally, there is no advantage to an official or his department in a weak politician. Officials do not like political heads who cannot exert influence or hold their own in competitions for resources with other departments through committees and the Cabinet. In central government the civil servants appreciate ministers who know their own minds, take few things for granted and are sensitive to political forces outside. Departments need ministers who can take decisions and win battles in Cabinet. Civil servants have their own views about what is important for the country and, recognising that they cannot act independently, look for strong ministerial leadership.

One conclusion that has been drawn from the web of interrelationships between officials and ministers in policy making is that the combination of limited ministerial power and the administrator's preference for conciliation leads to a 'directionless consensus' in British government.[56]

Interestingly the criticisms that have been made of the civil service have been aimed not at its political power but at its inadequate policy-planning. Recent changes in structures and methods of decision-making have been designed to strengthen departmental planning capabilities. So far as these succeed they will inevitably increase the power of officials in government. They will give that power more 'direction'. Ministers will find it even more difficult to resist the choice of policy options pressed on them by their official advisers if they are based on better analysis of the needs of the future, better long-term forecasting and better research carried out by administrators who are better trained in the relevant techniques of analysis.

The administrator, in other words, is called on increasingly to provide the rational element in the policy process. He is required to do better the very things that enhance his power. The next part of this book examines the methods of decision-making available to government organisations and the obstacles which stand in the way of them attaining all the characteristics of the rational model of decision-making and planning.

THE JUDICIARY IN THE POLITICAL PROCESS

The political experiences of some countries suggest that any consideration of power in the policy-making process and of constraints on the executive should include the role of the judiciary and its relationships with the executive branch of government. In the United States, for example, where the separation of powers is institutionalised to a greater extent than in Britain, the Constitution entitles the Supreme Court to exercise judicial review of legislation. Many judges in the lower courts are elected to office. Policies in many fields have been influenced by judicial decisions. Hence the interest among American political scientists in 'jurimetrics' or the quantitative analysis of the relationships between the socio-economic backgrounds of judges and their attitudes and decisions.

Under the rules and conventions of the British constitution, the judiciary seems to be highly politicised by the absence of a clear separation of powers. The country's most senior judge, the Lord

Chancellor, is both a member of the Cabinet and Speaker of the Upper House of the legislature. The highest court of appeal consists of five law lords appointed by the Lord Chancellor. The Prime Minister and Lord Chancellor select the judges to be appointed as Lords Justices and so form the Court of Appeal. The Queen, on the recommendation of the Lord Chancellor, appoints High Court judges and the Lord Chancellor appoints other judges, magistrates and chairmen of tribunals. As a senior minister, the Lord Chancellor is chosen by the Prime Minister. Do these interrelationships mean that the executive dominates the judiciary and therefore prevents it from acting as a constraint on executive power?

In fact, as is so often the case in British government, the constitution is not a completely reliable guide to political realities. The judiciary's role in the political process is a complex one. There are factors which protect it from the claims of the executive. But there are also factors which prevent this independence from leading to positive intervention in the government's policy-making functions. At the same time, however, there are some areas in which judicial decision-making does contribute to the formulation of policies; where judges use their discretion in the interpretation and development of legal rules and so contribute to the rule-making function of government as well as the adjudicatory function. The elements of this complexity are as follows.

First, a degree of independence is secured for the judiciary by constitutional convention. Judges' salaries are not open to discussion by Parliament. Since 1701 judges have been appointed until retirement and can only be dismissed by resolution of both Houses of Parliament. Such action has never been taken. Neither the Crown nor its ministers may exercise judicial functions. Judges are protected from legal action in their administration of justice so that it may be carried out without fear or favour. They are not under compulsion to obtain verdicts of guilty, but to ensure a fair hearing and to administer the law impartially.

Secondly, few judges have party political experience or a partisan background. Whereas in the nineteenth century some 65 per cent of judges were MPs when appointed, nowadays only about 9 per cent have had political experience, and then often only as an unsuccessful parliamentary candidate. There are few political offices in Britain compatible with judicial experience. Even the few who have some partisan attachment are as likely to be selected and promoted by their political adversaries as by their friends.[57]

Thirdly, the judiciary is neutralised by certain aspects of the political culture. It is assumed that in a parliamentary democracy judges will act as independent arbiters of disputes. Their role is to administer the law when conflicts arise in a neutral and impartial way. They are merely concerned with administering the law in relation to particular cases, and not with declaring on the merits or quality of legal rules. There is thus no judicial review of legislation. Parliament, not the courts, determines the scope of legislative power. Judges cannot test the validity of parliamentary enactment against some higher norm, unlike American Supreme Court justices who 'regularly test the validity of legislation against constitutional standards of which they are the guardians'.[58] The British courts accept the sovereignty of Parliament. No court since the seventeenth century has struck down an Act of Parliament for violating some fundamental principle. The training and socialisation of judges, as well as the climate of political opinion, further inhibits judicial review of English legislation. The courts generally hold themselves aloof from all types of conflicts within the political system.

Fourthly, the principle of precedent inhibits the judiciary from developing and changing the law by judicial interpretation. The importance of precedent reflects the judiciary's concern for the certainty of the law. Predictability is more important than reform to keep pace with changing values. Judges do participate in law reform, but through membership of specially appointed commissions. Law reform is not regarded as a legitimate function of adjudication, but of parliamentary legislation.

Finally, the courts have adopted a very precisely and narrowly defined role in cases of conflict between the citizen and the state. Here there are two main constraints. One is where a minister is given wide discretion to determine a case, such as when a statute empowers a minister to act in certain circumstances which in his judgement exist. Here it becomes virtually impossible to overrule his decision in defence of an aggrieved citizen. Such statutory powers were authorised by Parliament at least partly as a response to judicial hindrance of legislation in the 1920's and 30's.

The traditional reaction of judges to developments in executive power was to ensure that no public authority was allowed to act *ultra vires* and to see that executive powers were not exercised unfairly, unreasonably, in bad faith, on irrelevant grounds or for improper purposes. The application of such principles by conservative judges could and did affect the policy intentions of politicians and administrators.[59] The hostile attitude of judges to the development of the positive state has gradually been lessened, in the face of public demands for welfare and planning by parliamentary enactments which have strengthened the position of executive agencies by extending their discretionary powers. Thus the role of the judiciary in responding to administrative action has been to protect the common law rights of the citizen confronted with growing state power designed to defend the weak, the poor and the badly housed. Judges are more concerned with the procedural qualities of excutive decision making than with their substantive content, especially when those decisions have a quasi-judicial quality themselves.

It is symptomatic of the relationship between executive and judiciary that as an alternative to judicial review of administration the British system of government has used special tribunals for appeals against the discretionary decisions of the administration. Although tribunal procedures have been increasingly judicialised to meet the demands of natural justice, the executive's domination of policy-making has been protected by building an appeals procedure into the final stage of some administrative processes rather than allowing review by the courts.

The other major weapon in the executive's armoury against the courts is the doctrine of Crown privilege. The permits ministers to protect the internal communications of departments by confidentiality and thereby immunise the servants of the state against giving testimony and producing evidence when it is claimed by ministers that to do so would be detrimental to the interests of the state. Here again judges have had to decide on the right balance between state power and individual rights and liberties, and have had some success in reducing the scope of Crown privilege.[60] For example, the doctrine is no longer claimed as a matter of policy for police reports on road accidents, medical reports on civilian employees of the state or police statements.

In criticising Crown privilege the courts have claimed that the executive is not the sole guardian of the public interest. The courts also preserve part of that interest in seeing that justice is done. However the courts still maintain a distinction between the judgement of policy issues — a political responsibility — and the preservation of judicial values whenever the rights of individual citizens appear to be threatened by executive power.

In view of all these constraints on the development of judicial policy-making, is there any way in which the courts can be said to influence the formation of public policy? There are three aspects of judicial decision-making which must be included in any assessment of the policy process.

The first is the criminal law. This is created by judges in that the basis of criminal law is common law. What constitutes criminal conduct is determined by the courts. Parliament's efforts to improve the criminal law by statute have been built on common law. There is no criminal code. It is thus for the judges to decide whether a charge brought in the courts should be defined as a crime. For example, a conspiracy to corrupt public morals is only a crime because the judges say it is. The offence has no statutory definition. There is no Act of Parliament prohibiting it.[61]

Secondly, the treaties establishing the European Economic Communities are constitutional documents in that Parliament must accept the laws made under them. Community law will have to be interpreted and applied within the UK by British courts guided by the European Court, 'the ultimate and authoritative interpreter of the Treaties, and the regulations and directions of the Market'.[62] The British courts will be required to administer a body of public law derived from constitutional rules made independently of Parliament. Such laws may be in conflict with Parliament's statutes. The courts may also be required to pass judgement on the 'constitutional' validity of those statutes. In the European Court there is already a noticeable concern with the policy content of law. The British courts may well have to follow this lead and move from statutory interpretation to statute invalidation. Lord Justice Scarman has predicted that: 'Our courts, since they must accept the guidance of the European Court, will have to adopt a more positive continental approach to the policy of a measure when interpreting and applying it, and will have to overcome their native disposition to take refuge in the proposition that policy is not for the courts to consider.'[63]

Finally, by virtue of their class origins and life-style, judges are inevitably a conservative element in the political system.[64] It is noticeable that their concern to protect individual liberties has been less in evidence when it comes to the rights of working men to strike or peacefully picket, the rights of the poor to welfare assistance, the rights of immigrants to liberty and security, the rights of political refugees to asylum, the rights of women, the rights of the condemned to humane punishment, the rights of demonstrators to protest, or the rights of citizens generally if it happens to be a Conservative administration with which they find themselves in conflict. Lawyers generally (but with some notable exceptions) are the most conservative professionals, and display a bias in their attitudes and often in their decisions towards property owners and the wealthy. They support the power of the state when it is used to preserve the domination of such groups and oppose it when it attempts to redistribute resources and power in favour of the less privileged elements in society.

CHAPTER 7

Self-determination in the Localities

Both the study and practice of public policy-making are complicated by the devolution of power to local governments. Devolution produces a territorial pattern of geographical areas with important empirical features relevant to policy-making, the most important of which are demographic, social, economic and ideological. Each local government area is to some extent unique in terms of the size and social structure of the population, the economic activity of the area and the political values generated by these socio-economic factors.

Each local authority constitutes a miniature political and administrative system. Each has the institutions and processes of government — an electoral system, a legislative organ, appointed officials, party activity and conflict between individuals and groups over the allocation of resources and the enforcement of values. Local authorities are given powers under law to provide a specified range of services to local communities. They are multi-functional governments with all that implies by way of conflict and compromise in determining where the best interests of the community lie. A local government has to decide upon the right allocation of resources between competing claims. It will provide a mixture of services designed to meet the special needs of the area. These needs are established in a highly political manner. Devolution is politicised decentralisation.

Implied in devolution, therefore, is a degree of autonomy in policy-making. This is usually represented by an independent power to raise local revenues by taxation. Such revenues permit the discretion in meeting local needs from local resources which is considered a necessary condition of local self-government. Of course under devolution it is Parliament and thereby the government which creates the system of local government itself. It is within the constitutional power of Parliament to abolish all local authorities by the ordinary statutory process. The 1972 Local Government Act is a reminder of the extent to which local authorities are the creatures of Parliament. They can be abolished, merged or have their status changed by simple Act of Parliament.

Similarly it is up to Parliament to decide what powers local authorities will exercise. Local authorities in Britain can only do what Parliament authorises. Parliament, not the local authorities, determines whether or not local governments can provide their communities with health services, houses, drinking water, schools, sewage systems, roads or homes for old people. Each local government is thus subject to the doctrine of *ultra vires*. They are not only prevented from doing things which are expressly prohibited by law. They are also prevented from doing things that the law does not prescribe. The accounts of local authorities are subject to audit by central government inspectors who are required by law to disallow items of expenditure which are contrary to law. The District Auditor, under the supervision of the courts, is empowered to surcharge the amount of any such expenditure upon the persons responsible for incurring or authorising it. On rare occasions this power can impinge on policy-making within areas prescribed by law, since the District Auditor can surcharge on the grounds that expenditure was unreasonable or contrary to the interests of the local ratepayers.

These powers of central government over local authorities establish the parameters within which local policy-making has to be carried on. It does not follow that because the structure and powers of local authorities are determined by parliamentary statute, local authorities have no discretionary power to assess the needs of their communities and formulate a response to them. For this to be the case it would be necessary for the central government to control policy-making by local councils within those areas authorised by statute.

There is a school of thought which argues that such central controls do in fact impose a degree of uniformity on the local government system and restrict the autonomy of local councils to such an extent that they operate merely as the administrative agencies of central departments. If this were the case there would be no point in studying policy-making in local government, since it could not exist. Autonomy in any system of devolution is bound to be relative, but is it the case that local authorities perform a purely administrative role?

To answer this question adequately it is necessary to examine the political and administrative framework within which local authorities exist. Central government does exercise a range of controls over local government for a variety of reasons. These reasons and controls will be examined first to identify the factors which are likely to restrict local autonomy and which should therefore be included in any analysis of a specific authority or policy area. Then the picture of relative autonomy in local policy-making will be completed by an assessment of the factors which indicate and explain the ability of local authorities to respond individually and uniquely to the problems of their geographical areas.

CENTRAL CONTROL

Central control over local decision-making exists for two main reasons, one relating to the importance of individual local government services, the other to the importance of local government generally in the system of British government.

Some local government services have a national significance in that central governments have from time to time committed themselves politically to particular lines of development. Examples are education and housing. Where central government has decided for political reasons to determine national policies for a service administered by local authorities, such as prohibiting local education authorities from supplying school milk to children over seven, it will inevitably attempt to enforce such policies by controlling local decision-making. Local authorities may be entitled by law to provide certain services, but this is no guarantee that central government will have no policy on the matter. To a certain extent governments stake their political futures on developments for which local authorities share responsibility.

The political significance of some local government functions to central ministers is seen in the way minimum standards are enforced throughout the country. Central government decides that the national interest is served by ensuring that the quality of service is not markedly lower in some parts of the country than others, and consequently attempts to control decision-making to that effect. The standards concerned apply to the quality of construction works, the costs of projects, the quality of officials, the adequacy of service provision and the procedures by which authorities go about their business.[1]

The second reason for central control of local authorities is the importance of local government to the governmental system as a whole.

TABLE 7.1
Public expenditure by programme and spending authority 1971−2*

Programme	(a) Central government	(b) Local authorities	(c) Total	£ millions (b) as % of (c)
Defence	2,967		2,967	
Overseas service	382		382	
Agriculture etc	491	6	497	1.2
Research councils	134		134	
Trade, industry and employment	1,233	20	1,253	1.6
Roads	296	569	865	65.8
Transport	127	72	199	36.2
Housing	255	934	1,189	78.6
Public health and environmental	31	956	987	96.9
Law and order	162	603	765	78.8
Arts	26	9	35	25.7
Education	479	2,722	2,801	97.8
Health and social services	2,202	462	2,664	17.3
Social security	4,427		4,427	
Financial administration	279	26	305	8.5
Common services	255		255	
Miscellaneous	60	11	71	15.5
	13,806	6,390	19,796	32.3†

*Excluding public corporations, Northern Ireland and debt interest.
†Local government expenditure as a percentage of total expenditure is 29.3%

This importance can be expressed in terms of the range of services provided and the proportion of public expenditure which falls to local government. Table 7.1 shows the contribution which local government makes to the main functional categories of government activity. From this table it can be seen that 30 per cent of public expenditure is delegated to local government.

Local government expenditure thus has considerable economic significance. Local authorities are in competition for resources with both the private sector and other government bodies. Local government has been spending an increasing proportion of the national income since 1945. It accounts for over 20 per cent of total domestic investment. Its expenditure has been increasingly financed from Exchequer grants. Capital investment is funded by loans, and the extent of local authority borrowing is a factor which the Treasury must take into account when seeking to influence the money market. Each year local authorities are required by the central government to adjust their spending in the interest of national economic policy. Expenditure restrictions were called for in 1968 to release resources for improving the trade balance and avoiding inflation. In 1970, under a new Conservative administration, local authorities were asked to concentrate their resources on services which only they, and not the private sector, could provide. Government attempts to control inflation affect local authorities continuously. They have affected pay negotiations between local authorities and their employees. They have also affected the levels of local rates. So far as the government has a responsibility for regulating the economy, and therefore with competing claims on national resources, it must be directly concerned with the movement of total local government expenditure.

Local government spending is consequently planned as part of national public expenditure. The central government determines the rate of increase in local authority expenditure according to what it regards as the resources necessary to achieve the programmes set out in the annual White Papers on public expenditure. Local authorities are required to submit their estimates to the central departments. The total of these is used to determine the contribution which the Exchequer makes to local authority revenues (now running at approximately 40 per cent of local revenues). This contribution is based on existing levels of expenditure, prices and demand for services as well as any need to improve the quality of services. From this calculation the central government determines the level of specific grants which it makes to local authorities for particular services and the size of the Rate Support Grant, a general grant to support local revenue. Remaining expenditure must be met by local authorities' own tax revenues — the rates.

Within this broad framework of political and economic interest in local government on the part of central government, the central departments have developed a wide range of instruments by which they influence local council decisions. Local authorities are required by statute to prepare and submit plans for specified services for ministerial approval. Some individual decisions require central approval, such as loan sanctions. There are regulations prescribing how local authorities should perform certain duties. Some ministers are empowered to issue directives to individual authorities. There are statutes which permit ministers to declare a local authority in default in its provision of a service, and to make other arrangements for its administration. Ministers may become involved in local decision-making by acting in an adjudicatory capacity, either between local authorities or between an authority and a private citizen, as in the case of planning appeals.

Each of the above means of influence rests ultimately on legal sanction and therefore a power to control. There are other means of influence which are equally, if not more, important, but which do not imply coercion. There are important central inspectorates of local services, such as education. Ministers regularly and frequently send out circulars informing and advising local authorities of trends in government policies. They also advise and influence local government through the informal network of links between individual authorities, the local authority associations, individual ministers and their senior departmental officials.

As a consequence of all this it came to be believed very strongly that central control limited the autonomy of local authorities to such an extent that any diversity was virtually impossible. Local government, it was believed, had become the subservient agent of the central government. Accompanying this belief in the effect of central-local relationships was an assumption about the effect of population size on the efficiency of a local authority. Broadly, and for reasons which cannot be gone into here, it was assumed that the small authority was less efficient than the large and as a consequence was even more subject to central control. This was because smaller authorities would be even more dependent than larger ones on central funds and would, because of their inefficiencies, attract even greater ministerial supervision.[2] For our purposes it is the general assumption about the relationship of central government to all local authorities which is of greatest significance when considering the policy-making potential of local authorities. However the size-efficiency relationship is also important since it implies a differential policy-making potential within the local government system itself.

Recent investigations by political scientists into the factors which can be shown to be related in statistical terms to local government policies reveal that central control is by no means the dominant element. As one would expect in any self-governing territory, local authority policies are at least partly a function of local conditions and circumstances and the perceptions which local policy-makers have of them.

LOCAL POLICY-MAKING

Evidence supporting the view that central controls and pressures are not the major determinants of service provision is found in the fact that local authorities vary greatly in the amounts of money which they spend on such services as personal welfare, education and libraries. Statistical analysis of the effects on levels of expenditure and the allocation of financial resources within local authorities of central government grants reveals that 'the heavy financial dependence of British local authorities on central government has not produced a demonstrable effect on policy choice in the sub-national system', so that 'several of the more emotional arguments about central dominance of local affairs are exaggerated, if not totally incorrect'.[3] There is also the fact that variations in policies and levels of efficiency cannot be explained simply in terms of different population sizes and levels of wealth. Larger authorities do not consistently score higher standards of service provisions than smaller authorities.[4] The smaller and poorer authorities deviate considerably above and below the average level of expenditure for a particular service, a phenomenon not to be dismissed as the result of diseconomies of scale. Plans for the development of specific services, like levels of expenditure, reveal resistance to central control on the part of both large and small local authorities. Some explanation is clearly needed of the divergencies in policy-making to be found among local authorities responsible for service provision within the frameworks laid down by the central government.[5]

If local authority policy-making is not merely a product of population size, wealth and strong central control, there must be other factors which determine the 'authoritative allocations' made by local authorities.

One set of factors consists of the social, economic and physical characteristics of the communities to be governed. These are sometimes referred to as 'needs',[6] but this implies the application of values to community characteristics. Values differ, and what one policy-maker may regard as a need may not be so regarded by another. Nevertheless such characteristics have been shown to be related to policy outputs and so must be included in the analysis of local policy-making. It is also a fact that some 'needs' are created by external forces, and local authorities have to meet them. An example is compulsory education, which means that all education authorities must provide places for children aged between five and fifteen. The 'need' is created by the existence of such an age group combined with local government's statutory duty.

For example, in education policy-making social class composition shows a close relationship to spending, as well as, of course, the size of the population. Policy in the housing field, if measured in terms of the proportion of house building in an area carried out by the local council and the amount that the council decides the general population should contribute to the cost of housing council tenants, is closely related to social and physical factors. The social structure of the community, the availability of standard amenities in houses, and levels of overcrowding are all related to housing outputs. *Per capita* spending on the personal social services is affected by the social structure, age structure and density of the population and by housing standards. Among the protective services of local government *per capita* spending on the police appears to be increased in large, densely populated communities with relatively high property values. Spending on the fire service is affected by the proportion of the population in the lower social classes and its size, the larger authorities favouring lower fire service expenditure.[7]

The financial policies generally of local authorities are similarly conditioned by local characteristics. The larger the proportion of high social classes and high value domestic property, the lower the rate levied, reflecting a group interest in low taxation. The amounts which local authorities raise from their rates and their general levels of recurrent expenditure are both correlated with the social and economic structures of their areas as measured by the percentages of total rateable values coming from different sources — domestic, industrial, shops, offices and so on.[8]

For a socio-economic characteristic of the community to become a need to be met by public policies it must either be perceived by policy-makers as a problem, or imposed from outside by some statutory obligation requiring local authorities to deal with specified situations in specified ways. Neither community characteristics nor imposed obligations are incompatible with the theory that local government is dominated by central government. It is not until characteristics are perceived as problems, or statutory obligations become open to discretionary interpretation or extension beyond minimum requirements, that opportunities for the exercise of local power are created. The variable effect of political values on local decisions must be

demonstrated to prove that local government is not centrally dominated. 'Political' is used here in the broadest sense of choosing between
alternative lines of action in order to achieve some goal which is
regarded as desirable. Political values may thus be as much a part of the
official's as the politician's decision-making.

Research has shown that local political variables do affect the way in
which needs are perceived and met. Indeed many of the social
characteristics of the population which appear to be directly related to
policy outputs have proved, on closer inspection, to be a function of
intervening variables measuring some aspect of political decision-
making. For example, council spending on the police appears to be a
function of social class composition but on more detailed investigation
turns out to be related to the type of party control found in
middle class areas. Again in the case of the library service expenditure is
not so much related to 'needs', or likely demand generated by the class
and age structure of the population, as by the involvement in
decision-making by organised groups within the community.[9]

The political strengths and attitudes of local communities have been
shown to be related to policy outputs in a number of ways, although it
is difficult to single out the influence of the political composition of
councils from the socio-economic structure of the electorates which
produce them. Oliver and Stanyer, for example, measured political
strengths and attitudes as the percentage of council seats held by the
Labour Party, and related this to the financial behaviour of county
boroughs. They found that significant relationships between financial
variables and the strength of the Labour Party were almost entirely
explained by the connections between the socio-economic structures of
the boroughs and Labour Party electoral success.[10] Boaden, on the
other hand, in a study of reorganisations in authority management
structures and changes in secondary education policy, found Conservative councils much more ready than Labour to alter their committee
arrangements and Labour councils more likely than Conservative to
reorganise secondary education along comprehensive lines. These cases
were offered as 'clear evidence of the impact of elected members. In
both they exercise considerable independent impact ... Political
control will affect the patterns of activity and the rate of change.'[11]

Boaden's research also shows that party control affects levels of
spending. Labour councils were found to spend more on education and
to build more council houses than Conservative councils. Labour-
controlled councils also pay higher subsidies in the housing field than

other councils, whatever the extent of need or the availability of resources.[12] Labour control was also found to have a distinct but differential effect on social service spending, while Conservative councils are likely to spend more proportionately on the police than Labour 'as befits their law and order traditions'.[13] Before they were taken over by the Area Health Authorities there was a 'consistent, positive and generally significant correlation between Labour representation and spending on local health services'.[14]

The response of policy-makers to the needs created by their perceptions of local circumstances is mediated through the resources available for problem solving. Research into the variable effect of resources, measured in terms of *per capita* rateable values and rates levied, shows that poorer authorities spend proportionately more than the larger ones. It is well known that in local government the less wealthy communities pay higher local taxes to support the services which they need: 'The poor are big spenders and consequently big taxers.'[15] Dependence on central government grants, although helping to maintain standards in the poorer authorities, does not impose uniformity in local government spending by removing the need for some authorities to impose relatively higher taxes on their ratepayers than others.

Research using aggregate data for the comparison of local government policy-making has to be interpreted cautiously and accurately. It should not be taken to demonstrate more than it claims for itself. There are some methodological difficulties to be overcome, as is readily accepted by the researchers working in this field.

First, there is the problem of distinguishing between and giving some sort of weighting to the effects of national and local variables. The relative effects of central grants and local revenues on service provision is an example of the difficulty. Such variables can be quantified and their relationships to output measured statistically. The problem is even greater if an attempt is made to measure the less direct influences of central on local government.

Second, there are the problems of assessing the relative impact of local variables, such as political attitudes and dispositions, the availability of local resources and the socio-economic characteristics of the community. In the case of the fire service, for example, it has been found that working class communities spend more than middle class ones. Does this mean that the working class is favourably disposed towards the service, perhaps as an expression of local, working class pride? Or is fire service spending related to the degree of trade unionism found in the service, which itself would be related to class composition? Or is the level of spending a function of the relatively low cost of the service combined with the poor council's entitlement to differentially higher central grants? Or does the spending reflect the Labour Party's sensitivity to its electoral support? Or are Labour councils associated with fire service spending because of their association with working class communities?[16] The problem of locating the dependent and independent variables is not easily solved.

Third, there is the problem of devising reliable indicators of inputs and outputs and, therefore, of interpreting the statistical relationships which might be demonstrated. For example, it is widely accepted that groups other than the politicians play a role in policy-making. But how can the contributions of officials and organised interests be measured? Can the number of committees or the employment of an O and M officer be taken as a satisfactory indicator of official influence? Does the existence of capital budgeting indicate official autonomy, suggesting as it does long-term planning which favours the power of officials at the expense of parties and individual councillors?[17]

The influence of the community other than through its elected representatives is also not easily measured, since there are so few quantitative indicators of community involvement which are readily available. Information of attitudes and political activities must be collected through survey methods which are expensive. The level of turnout at local elections is only a very rough and ready guide to local interest and involvement, and it is perhaps not surprising Boaden found that turnout as a measure of public impact on service provision, was not statistically related to outputs.

Turning to the output side of the political process, it is equally difficult to find reliable indicators of differences in public policies. Variation in expenditure per head of population over a number of local authorities for a given service may be used. But the results must be interpreted cautiously. Similar levels of expenditure may conceal differences in the prices of commodities available to authorities, in their levels of efficiency in the use of resources, and in the way they collect and record data on service provision.[18] Some attempt must be made to build these variables into the model.

The problem can be further illustrated from the social services, one of local government's most important functions. Great care must be exercised in the interpretation of such variables as the proportion of children in care or boarded out, the total number of children helped by the authority, the proportion of welfare officers with relevant qualifications, the ratio of old people receiving local authority domestic help to the number resident in old people's homes, or the number of old people receiving services.[19] The interpretation of these variables may be more important when making value judgements about the quality of services than when calculating the political causes of policy outputs simply to show the significance of purely local factors. Nevertheless the two considerations can never be entirely separated. The choice of input measures, such as party composition of the local council, is determined by expectations about the intentions of different political groups and organisations, such as that Conservatives will be more favourably disposed towards expenditure on cultural amenities than Labour councillors. If such hypotheses are to be tested convincingly it is important to know whether the measure of output chosen really reflects the values under investigation. For example, before associating the number of old people placed in homes and institutions with some political factor (and perhaps blaming some group for it) it is important to know whether the proportion is the accidental outcome of the capital stock of institutional places available.[20]

None of the above points are intended as criticisms of this type of research. Indeed it is one of the two most important types of investigation being carried out into local government and politics (the other being into the appropriateness of organisational structures for the management of different tasks, a subject outside the scope of this book). It raises interesting methodological problems and increases our understanding of political relationships.[21] But most important of all, it corrects a misconception about the autonomy of local authorities as policy-*making* bodies. It can no longer be assumed that central control creates uniformity throughout the country and that local factors are unimportant in the formulation of policy. Nor can it be assumed that where variations in policy-making exist, they are explained simply by divergencies of size and local resources. Poor local authorities are helped disproportionately by central grants to finance expensive services like education. But the way the money is used is a response to local pressures. For a full understanding of the policy-making process local authorities must, it seems, be treated as 'authoritative allocators'. 'The centre has a part to play in setting boundaries within which local authorities operate, but the divergence within those boundaries must be explained elsewhere.'[22]

PART III

CHAPTER 8

Objectives and Alternatives

Chapter 3 identified the elements of a rational decision-making process which could be applied to policy-planning in government. It was suggested that there are three main problem areas which confront the planner in any attempt to improve the rationality of planning. The first is the specification of both short and long term objectives, the means of reaching them and the expression of those means in financial or budgetary terms. Also in this problem area is the function of review, that is the evaluation of the objectives achieved with the means employed. The growing concern in government organisations with the problem of objectives is reflected in the adoption and adaptation of planning methods used by foreign governments and British industry.

More and more local authorities, for example, are engaging in some form of corporate planning. Local government has been accused of giving too much attention to operating services and too little to planning them. Authorities have been urged to reject their 'ingrained departmental approach' to management and adopt a corporate approach 'to ensure that their resources are most effectively deployed'. A corporate approach entails making 'a realistic attempt to plan ahead on an authority-wide basis, to formulate objectives, evaluate alternative methods of achieving those objectives and measure the effectiveness of ultimate performance against those objectives.'[1] It has even been suggested that 'corporate planning runs the danger of becoming the thing no self-respecting local authority should admit to being without'.[2]

In 1973 the Permanent Secretary of the Department of Education and Science contributed to a lecture series on 'corporate planning' organised by the Royal Institute of Public Administration. He started by saying, 'I don't know whether my Department does corporate planning,' and then went on to describe educational planning in terms which revealed a close similarity of approach.[3] Corporate planning has also been introduced into the British Gas Corporation. It has been defined by its Member for Economic Planning as 'a disciplined study to determine the long and short term objectives of the organisation as a whole — together with the constraints which limit its course of action — and to devise a practical plan to achieve those objectives'.[4] The economic planning division at the headquarters of the British Gas Corporation has a director of corporate planning. The division initiates the preparation of a corporate plan submitted to the Secretary of State for Energy each year and covering all major operations on a rolling five year basis.

While some organisations refer to their methods of policy-making as corporate planning, others with more diverse ranges of activities have introduced output budgeting, or planning, programming, budgeting (PPB) systems, into various parts of the organisation as a procedure for expenditure planning appropriate to government. PPB 'is a planning system in which expenditures are displayed in a way which relates them to major policy objectives and in which analysis is carried out on the cost and benefits of alternative routs to those objectives'.[5]

For example, PPB has been introduced into the management of individual police forces for reasons typically associated with rational planning in public service agencies. Information about resources has traditionally been classified in terms of goods and services rather than programmes or activities. Information about police effectiveness in reaching stated objectives (and therefore efficiency) has been misleading or non-existent. PPB has therefore been introduced to 'provide policy authorities, Chief Constables and the Home Secretary with more and better information about their policy options by enabling them to look for the first time at expenditure in terms of programmes as well as inputs. In this way, it will provide a formal mechanism for relating expenditure more closely to recognised social needs'.[6]

A recent development in British central government designed to improve policy-planning is a system of programme analysis and review (PAR). The motive behind PAR is similar to that behind PPBS: to increase the rationality of decision-making 'involving choices by responsible departments of the best means of achieving the ends they exist to accomplish, or of supplying the services they have to provide'.[7] PAR links planning and review by analysing established policies to see whether they are still justified. It seeks to apply techniques of cost appraisal and measurement to alternative methods of achieving determined objectives. Programmes are chosen for analysis and review by joint discussions between the departments, the Treasury and the Central Policy Review Staff. Ideally all government activities should be subject to PAR, and the reviews would be completed in time to feed into the PESC exercise (see below).[8] However so far this has proved physically impossible. A selective and experimental approach has been adopted, so that improvements in decision-making within departments have yet to make much impact on interdepartmental or strategic choices.

THE ANALYSIS OF OBJECTIVES

Corporate planning, PAR and PPBS are all centred around one dominant problem area: policy objectives. They focus on a set of related questions about the objectives of an organisation: what is the organisation trying to achieve?; how can the objectives be reached? what does it cost to reach them?; have they in fact been reached after the costs have been incurred?[9] Ultimately these questions have to be posed and answered in financial terms. Budgeting and planning become intertwined. But the principles underlying the budgetary process are simply those of rationality and efficiency expressed in terms of cost effectiveness. As Professor Alan Williams said in an influential pamphlet on the subject: 'The basic idea of an output budget is to relate all cost items to broad functional objectives, by constructing a framework within which it is clear what resources are being devoted towards what end and with what result.'[10]

Government organisations which adopt this approach to policy-planning set themselves three difficult analytical tasks: specifying objectives, costing programmes and monitoring progress.

The specification of functional objectives

The first task of an organisation is to establish its aims and objectives, as far as possible in measurable and quantifiable terms. Time limits must also be specified. 'An objective should be measurable. It should state the quantity (and quality, if possible) of benefit that is being aimed at and the period in which it is to be provided.'[11] Measurable objectives enable performance criteria to be developed, so that reviews can assess the effectiveness of chosen policies. It follows that objectives have to move from the vague and ambiguous to the precise and quantifiable. For example, the objective 'to provide the highest possible standard of education, according to the child's age, aptitude and ability' has to be broken down into measures or indicators of success, such as reading and mathematical ability, examination results, social adjustment indicators, school inspectors' assessments and so on.[12] It can readily be seen that the movement from a broad objective to specific measures of its attainment is a value-laden process and requires the exercise of political choice.

Clearly objectives must be specified in terms of the ends to be achieved rather than the means of achieving them. Objectives must not be confused with activities and expenditure. In local government, for example, an objective in housing might be 'to ensure that there is a sufficiency of new dwelling units and associated facilities to meet the changing needs of the area'. The activities leading to this objective could be identified as the direct provision of new dwellings, hostels and caravan sites; mortgage loans and grants to housing associations; and the sale or lease of land for private development.[13]

From these examples it can be seen that the specification of objectives in operational terms forces the planner to assess the needs of the community to be affected by changes in policy. No test of effectiveness or efficiency is possible unless the planner knows what impact he wishes to make on the community. If, for example, the effectiveness of housing policy is to be measured by the number of households housed rather than the number of dwellings built, it is imperative to assess the housing needs of the community.

Costing programmes

A number of related activities go towards achieving any given objective in government. The costs of these have to be identified so that resources used (or inputs) can be related to the level of objective achieved (output) and thereby provide a measure of efficiency. Hence the budgeting stage of rational planning is concerned with the allocation of expenditure to activities associated with known outputs.

For this reason an important part of output budgeting is the reclassification of accounts from the conventional government estimates to programme categories. It is well known that British governments traditionally present their expenditure plans by means of estimates of input costs, such as salaries, travel expenses, maintenance costs, rents, superannuation and sundry other expenses. If the value of expenditure has to be calculated by what it is achieving, however, resources must be analysed according to purpose and results. The planner must know what resources, or inputs, must be committed to the activities which are judged to contribute to the objectives of the organisation. Allocating expenditure according to the purposes for which the money is spent makes it possible to calculate the effects of changing priorities in expenditure and the costs of the results of each governmental activity.

Ideally the output or programme budget combines functional with traditional input or supply costings. For example, the Home Office function of 'treatment of offenders' has to be broken down into its programme costs (apprehension, detention, trial, training, rehabilitation and research) and into the supply costs of the police, courts, prison service, probation service, public works and so on.[14] This enables the planner to avoid confusing the level of inputs with the quality of service or effectiveness of function. For example, the ratio of medical staff to hospital beds ceases to be a measure of quality and becomes one among many inputs contributing to the desired objectives. The objective of, say, reducing mortality and morbidity rates can be related to variations in the use of all resources. In this way the vital element of choice between alternative programmes is introduced into the policy process.

Although output and input elements should be combined in the budgeting stage, it is imperative that the activities leading to specified objectives are not confused with the traditional categories for the supply estimates. This is likely to happen where, as in foreign affairs, it is difficult to define the activities or programmes in a way which relates them to objectives. For example, diplomatic service costs, subscriptions to international organisations and defence assistance are all related to the Foreign Office objective of maintaining the continuing security of the UK. But as expenditure categories they provide no information at all on the effectiveness or efficiency of the activities which they support. They do not even specify the activities as programme elements in a functional budget.

As well as departing from the categories of the supply estimates, output budgets are also concerned with longer time spans. They set out forward projections of programme costs so that it is clear what commitments are being made for the future. It has long been recognised that the annual appropriations of the traditional supply procedure in central government are inadequate for expenditure planning which requires up to, and sometimes in excess of, ten year projections. In 1961 the Plowden Committee recommended that regular forecasts should be made of public expenditure over a number of years ahead. As a consequence the Public Expenditure Survey Committee was set up in 1961, comprising the principal finance officers of the major central departments and chaired by a deputy secretary of the Treasury. PESC is responsible for showing ministers where existing policies will lead in terms of public expenditure at constant prices if they are maintained over the following five years. The PESC report is submitted to ministers along with the Treasury's medium-term assessment of the economy.[15]

Many policies imply commitments for the future, such as national insurance schemes and major capital programmes for power stations, roads and hospitals. Others take many years to produce desired changes, as in the time lag between expanding the teacher training programme and increasing the number of teachers in the classroom. Every programme must be projected forward so that its future demands on resources can be predicted. The main purpose of the exercise is to enable ministers to see where present policies will lead. They can then consider the economic prospects and decide whether the forecasts of demands upon resources made by the public sector need to be increased, left unchanged, or diminished. Ministers should also be able to decide whether the allocation of resources is in accordance with their own economic, social and political priorities.

Monitoring progress

The planning cycle is completed with the review of past activities and their success, relative to alternative possibilities, in achieving specified objectives. At the same time the objectives themselves will be reviewed[16] in the light of information about the costs of achieving them. The quality of this stage of the process depends upon the extent to which community needs have been expressed in measurable terms and the outputs of government policy related to them. Programme review also includes special studies of alternative methods of achieving given ends, such as reducing road accidents by traffic management, street lighting, physical alteration of highways, road safety education and so on. It is here that the planner needs reliable information to reduce uncertainty about the costs of alternative activities designed to satisfy some community need or solve some socio-economic problem. This is the subject of the next chapter.

OBSTACLES TO RATIONALITY

When thinking in purely abstract terms few would deny the need for government organisations to analyse objectives, consider alternative means to given ends and measure success rates. Yet there are many obstacles to the realisation of the degree of rationality implied in the theory of corporate planning, programme budgeting and PAR. Planners in Britain are aware of many of them, mainly because of false starts elsewhere. To be aware of the problems, however, is not to solve them. The problems associated with the analysis of government objectives may be usefully considered under the following headings: technical, administrative and political.[17]

Technical problems

First, the statistical information and theoretical models required for programme budgeting and review are expensive to acquire. The problem of information generally is explored in a later chapter, but it is important to note here that even when existing data can be reclassified for an output budgeting system it can sometimes require the sorting by computer of thousands of items of data.

Secondly, considerable difficulties have been encountered in deciding on a price basis for costing policies and programmes over a period of time. Technically it is very difficult to make sure that the correct price adjustments are made. Constant prices undervalue the real cost of expenditure programmes. More work needs to be done to produce a historical series of expenditures on a common basis. More information is needed on how price movements affect different expenditure programmes. 'Only in this way can one approximate to a measure of the real cost in objective or physical terms of a particular service.'[18]

Thirdly, the trained personnel and data processing equipment required for programme analysis are in short supply. Some departments are able to organise it as an extension of existing information and policy work. Others need additional staff or have to buy in outside consultants. In central government output budgeting is likely to develop first in those departments where the accounts can be relatively easily restructured into a programme budget, or where there are already staff to carry out the special analytical studies needed, or where costs and benefits are more easily measurable — for example, in a highways department rather than an education department.[19] The decision to implement PAR on a piecemeal basis, mentioned above, was partly caused by the shortage of appropriate skills and experience within departments.

> Analysis in depth of the problems under examination makes a big demand on existing resources. Training facilities have to be expanded. New costing systems have to be invented and appropriate measures devised of the results to be expected from the various options identified. So far the additional resources alloted to PAR have been comparatively modest though they are already putting a strain on departments which is bound to grow. This is likely to be the principal constraint on the development of PAR since there are distinct limits to the speed with which expert and experienced staff can be produced.[20]

When this situation is combined with strong political pressures to reduce the rate of increase in public expenditure, demands for additional planning staff are likely to be refused.

Fourthly, outputs in government are often difficult to quantify, making the success or failure of a programme correspondingly difficult to assess. In the public sector generally there are often no figures directly comparable to the value of sales or profits in the private sector. Output may be measurable, but difficult to value, as in the case of the Patent Office, the Ministry of Overseas Development and the Employment Service. Government agencies, and particularly the Treasury, are working on unit costs, management ratios and the adaptation of commercial accounting procedures to certain appropriate government functions in an effort to provide reliable methods 'of assessing administrative or managerial performance in situations where the simple yardstick of profitability is either inapplicable or insufficient'.[21] There is also the problem of weighting the different outputs of a public service — examination results versus 'social adjustment' in education, for example.[22]

Fifthly, the resources of public services often serve more than one purpose or objective. This can make it difficult to attribute costs. Experience of PPBS in local government suggests that: 'A programme area is best seen as a major focus of attention with fuzzy limits rather than a self-contained set of objectives and activities.'[23] Government programmes are not mutually exclusive, with each programme contributing to only one objective. It may be necessary to identify the marginal costs of the different objectives in order to consider trade-offs between the different uses of a given resource.[24] In defence the problem of apportioning the costs of general purpose military forces among the various commitments they might be called on to discharge is particularly acute.[25] Similarly it is not possible to determine how much of the expenditure incurred in restoring a person to health by hospital care contributes to the economic objective of minimising the loss of output or the social objective of minimising pain and disability.[26] The broader and more vague the objective, the wider the range of activities which can reasonably be seen as contributing to it.

This leads to the final technical problem, that of relating the intermediate objectives which can be precisely defined and costed to more general objectives. For example, improvements in staff-pupil ratios in schools must be critically reviewed from time to time from the point of view of their contribution to improved education. Whilst it is clearly important not to allow rational planning to get bogged down in fruitless distinctions between ends and means, it is equally important not to confuse the two and permit means to become ends in themselves. The specification of clear 'intermediate objectives' therefore becomes important. For example, to prevent a motorway network becoming an end in itself as a reaction against the vague objective of 'improving the economic and social well-being of the community', motorways have to be considered as one means of achieving better transport by reducing costs and accidents.

It is therefore necessary to select a level of objectives to be taken as the basis for analysis, avoiding on the one hand the Scylla of pitching the objectives too low and so restricting the range of alternatives considered, and on the other hand the Charybdis of pitching them too high so that they are too vague and the range of alternatives is too vast to be meaningful for analysis.[27]

Administrative problems

The first administrative problem is created by the machinery of government. Objectives are difficult to define and even more difficult to pursue when more than one administrative agency is involved. When local authorities share the provision of a service another political dimension is added. The sharing of functions between central and local government probably produces the greatest problems of expenditure planning and control. But there are also objectives to which, in central government, different functional and geographical departments contribute, e.g. Home Office and Scottish Home and Health Department responsibilities for the protection of persons and property and the treatment of offenders. Even greater complications arise when a private sector is involved. In education, for example, output budgeting 'probably ought to embrace the private sector as well, both because of the interaction between the two sectors and because Government decisions can affect in various ways the volume of national resources devoted to the private sector'.[28] Coupled with the problem of ensuring consistency of objectives when combining expenditures of different agencies in an output budget is that of management control, referred to below.

The dispersal of services at local community level among two tiers of elected authorities and appointed bodies such as health and water authorities and new town corporations, presents a special problem to those who look forward to a time when community planning can be carried on. 'Community planning is a concept, a notion intended to give expression to *community* objectives and policies, to provide a framework for all agencies having an impact on a community to plan their activities.'[29] Securing the necessary cooperation in the setting of interrelated objectives and the monitoring of progress will be a truly formidable task. Little progress has been made so far. It is ironic that at the same time as local government is beginning to recognise the interdependence of departmental corporate and physical planning, central government is insisting that community services such as health, water and drainage be hived off to quasi-autonomous, special purpose appointed bodies.

The development of plans and budgets on the basis of outputs and objectives can overcome some of these administrative difficulties. For this to happen, however, it is important that strategic planning systems be used in similar ways by different organisations. Thus it may be possible to avoid the problems which have occurred in other countries where PPBS has been regarded in different ways, sometimes as a planning technique, sometimes as a device for financial control and accounting.

The structures of programme budgets will of course vary from organisation to organisation, even when working in the same field. In education, for example, local authority decision-making requires a different programme structure to that of the Department of Education and Science. But different structures can produce mutually useful information. The Home Office, for example, has produced a programme budgeting system for police forces which is of value both to local management and the central department itself.

A second administrative problem area is that of organising planning in government agencies. The subject of management structures and methods for rational planning and control is a very large one. It would need a separate book to deal adequately with the relevance of accountable management, management by objectives and other methods to the kind of planning and budgeting systems discussed here. All that can be noted is the difficulty often encountered in government organisations in matching structures, and therefore control systems, to programmes. Many programmes cut across organisational boundaries, and many organisations are responsible for a variety of activities related to different objectives.[30] While an output budget can bring the expenditure activities of different institutions together and so enhance policy-planning, it becomes correspondingly limited for ensuring that actual expenditure coincides with plans, since such a control function must correspond to organisational structures.[31] Output budgeting in the police, however, is being developed on the basis of a common structure for planning and management.[32] In local government, too, corporate planning methods require corporate management structures, and the traditional departmental and committee systems are being reorganised in many authorities to reflect new processes of policy-planning.[33]

Finally, there is the problem of integrating the planning activities of individual agencies into a strategy for the government as a whole. The idea that the government should have a basic strategy and established priorities was made explicit in 1970. The Central Policy Review Staff was set up to identify policy areas in which choice could be exercised and to ensure that the underlying implications of alternative courses of action are fully analysed and considered.

This is a formidable task, logically implied by the development of the whole public expenditure survey system. There are disagreements between the spending departments and the Treasury on what constitutes 'existing policy' for the PESC exercise.[34] There is disagreement about the price basis for costing policies that are agreed upon. The projections based on disputed policies also give rise to disagreements especially when they depend on predictions of the unpredictable.

To this must be added the inescapable features of Cabinet government. Priorities are settled *ad hoc* by ministerial bargaining: 'Most Cabinet bargaining is a sequential operation in which major expenditures are each considered serially rather than all together at the same time.'[35] Comparisons of alternative uses of resources are therefore difficult for the government collectively to make. A recent thorough investigation of British public expenditure planning concluded that programme analysis and review followed rather than determined decisions about the allocation of resources. One object of PAR is to enable ministers and officials to compare the programmes of all departments. 'Nothing about PAR has even begun approaching this ideal.'[36]

The CPRS is regarded with suspicion by the departments, the Treasury and the Cabinet Office. Cabinet decisions so often have to be taken quickly, before analysis can be carried out. The CPRS is criticised as having failed to produce a broad strategy to replace the existing policies of which it is so often critical.

None of this should come as too much of a surprise if the political constraints on rational policy-making are considered. Indeed the administrative problems which have just been considered overlap extensively into political matters. The line between them is by no means clear in real life. Nor should it be surprising in view of the volume of public expenditure — 24,000 million or 50 per cent of GNP — and the vast range of public authorities of different types responsible for its planning and control.

Political problems

Firstly the clear and unambiguous specification of objectives required by pure rationality is impossible in politics where goals are determined by the interaction of many different political structures. Corporate planning and output budgeting offer no guidance on whose objectives should be used for the basis of analysis and execution. Only the political system can do this, and it by no means does it unambiguously. Different political groups (including groups of senior officials) will evaluate the costs and benefits of different courses of action in different ways.

Secondly, there is the fact that a greater reliance on policy analysis in the governmental process will increase the power of the analyst. Since the setting of objectives cannot be separated from consideration of the means to achieving them, it is not possible to assume that the analyst can be kept as the passive instrument of the politician. The definition of objectives in government is not just a difficult exercise intellectually. It also involves social and political values: PPB, for example, is not merely a neutral, technical exercise.[37]

Finally, future levels and patterns of public expenditure, and therefore the design of public policies, are heavily influenced by past patterns. It has been estimated that ministers have at the most a margin of 2½ per cent in any one year in which they can affect expenditure:

> The margin for real ministerial power in expenditure decisions is seriously limited because most of the total sum is predisposed. There are statutory commitments that are unquestioned as ongoing policies, and there is the natural growth of existing policies which expand in line with the population of beneficiaries or consequent decisions that had to be made by virtue of already existing decisions.[38]

The pattern of past decisions is the basis upon which only incremental changes can be built without a radical change of political values.

Educational planning at central government level provides a useful example of this constraint. The provision of compulsory educational facilities is dominated by basic demographic factors, that is, the expenditure required for existing numbers plus provision for expected growth and movements in the population. Also within the compulsory system changes in expenditure will be incurred by 'participation' changes, that is an increase or decrease in the proportion of the age group participating in the educational system or attending a particular type of institution. Even improvements in the quality of education are determined more by the output of teachers from training colleges, for example, than by deliberate reallocations of resources by policy-makers. In higher education, on the other hand, policy determinants include the extent to which policy-makers are prepared to find resources as well as the number of students wishing to study and possessing the required qualifications.[39]

RATIONAL POLICY-MAKING

Despite the limitations involved, corporate planning, PAR, PESC and PPBS are all in principle suggested by commonsense as things that all organisations with scarce resources should do: clarify objectives, devise efficient means of reaching them, assess performance and discover the costs of different projects.

However observations of policy- and decision-making in government confirm what has been experienced in all large organisations: that considerable modifications of the rationality model are called for while maintaining it as an ideal.

Decision-making models suggest the existence of a lone decision-maker. In government however decisions cannot be attributed to single individuals. Many groups contribute to decisions and they have different values. There is no 'rationally best' solution objectively provable to all. Conflicting interests do not see it as their responsibility even to try to work out the probable consequences of an infinite number of policy alternatives.

The model also suggests a neat division between ends (values) and means (instrumentals). But final ends (or goals) are rarely specified and all intermediate ends can be seen as means to some higher end. Thus there is no clear distinction in policy-making between fact and value.

Factors other than rationality determine which problems or which aspects of a problem are tackled by the decision maker. Priorities may be determined by the Gresham's law of decision-making — daily routine drives out planning — or by anticipation of reactions from superiors. When difficult decisions have to be made rational calculation may be rejected in favour of the convenience of routine formulae. The decision-maker's response to a situation may be to take no decision rather than undermine his own power or authority.

It is beyond the decision-maker's power to set out all policy alternatives with the probabilities of their consequences. Choices are inevitably arbitrary to some extent. This is because the decision-maker's information about his environment is at best an approximation to the real environment. A reason is that in large organisations (e.g. government departments) the search for solutions to problems is inevitably fragmented. Members of the organisation perceive limited aspects of the relevant information and have to communicate it to other decision-makers. Consequently decision-makers 'satisfice' rather than maximise. That is they do not necessarily seek the maximum utility (e.g. profitability in a firm). They may be content with a lower level of goal attainment. In addition individual values may not coincide with organisational values. Individual biases can influence problem-solving in organisations. They even influence the perception of the problem. Such biases arise from the interests and past experiences of decision-makers. The problems associated with information for policy-making are the subject of Chapter 10.

In comparing strategies it is necessary to calculate the probability of events occurring. Probabilities indicate risks to be taken. Two decision-makers may agree on the objective probability but only one may be prepared to take the risk because of different values. There may also be uncertainty about the probable outcome of a policy. Information reduces uncertainty and converts it into certainty or at least risk. But information may be costly and the decision-maker may decide to reduce uncertainty only up to a point below certainty. This may lead to the 'satisficing' mentioned above. Techniques to deal with risk and uncertainty are discussed in the next chapter.

CHAPTER 9

Costs and Benefits

In Chapter 3 it was shown that one of the tasks of the rational policy-maker is to compare alternative courses of action likely to solve a problem. In seeking the most efficient course of action the policy-maker needs to be fully informed of the consequences of each. To provide such information he needs to apply techniques of appraisal to different projects which will reduce his uncertainty about their implications for all those aspects of society in which he is interested.

There are many analytical techniques now being applied in the policy-planning sections of government organisations, such as operations research, cost-benefit analysis and systems analysis. The policy-planner uses them to select the optimum solution according to some specified criterion of effectiveness, whether expressed in terms of financial returns or some non-financial measures. Operations research, for example, has been used by the Home Office to determine the optimal distribution of police stations, by the Department of Education and Science to produce a computerised model of the whole educational system and by the Department of Employment in the planning of employment services in large cities. Cost-benefit analysis has been widely used in government, both central and local, on such projects as the siting of an international airport, the extension of underground railways, land conservation, motorway planning, forestry development, military defence and passenger transport fares. Nationalised industries are not only required to operate on a commercial basis and secure a rate of return on new investment specified by the government, they are also required to carry out cost-benefit analysis when the social costs or benefits of their investment projects are expected to diverge markedly from those associated with alternative investments.[1] Government agencies in general are required to develop better methods of measuring and comparing the cost-effectiveness of alternative courses of action in the planning of economic, social and community services.[2]

Although the available techniques of analysis vary considerably, a common objective underlies all of them. They are all concerned with determining the full implications of different strategies so that preferences can be expressed under conditions of complexity, change and conflicting values. Grouped together the techniques can be seen to relate to a number of interconnected problems.

ASPECTS OF ANALYSIS

Boundaries

First, there is the problem of identifying the boundaries of analysis, beyond which consideration of a project's effects has to be abandoned. This may be because of time, cost or technical difficulties or because effects beyond the boundary are ruled out as irrelevant to the project under analysis. One of the virtues of a cost-benefit approach to policy-analysis is that it requires the policy-maker to include in his calculations what might have been unforeseen consequences, either desirable or undesirable. In this way the full costs and benefits (in financial and other terms) to the community of otherwise accepted phenomena may be revealed. The effects of political values on resource allocation can thus be made more explicit.

For example, the planner is forced to consider the benefits of less mental and physical strain gained from motorway travel and compare them with damage to the environment and amenity, reckoned as costs. Externalities, social costs or spillover effects such as these are central to cost-benefit analysis. Other examples are the ecological effects of forestry, the effects of industry on amenity and clean air, the noise 'cost' of an international airport and the loss of life and amenity incurred by increases in road traffic.

Since the number of externalities of a project is virtually unlimited it is necessary to decide, perhaps somewhat arbitrarily, where the line is to be drawn between a viable and practicable piece of analysis and a full social appraisal which would be a 'piece of utopianism' and impossible to achieve.[3] Cost-benefit analysis in transport studies, for example, usually excludes the effects of projects on other than the users of transport facilities. Nevertheless this approach to policy-making reveals much more than is shown on a typical balance sheet. For example forestry policy affects recreational facilities, amenity, water supply, ecology, soil strucure and local employment. None of this is reflected in the low financial rate of profit shown on the Forestry Commission's accounts.[4]

Costs and benefits

The second problem is that of making economically rational choices where there is no price mechanism to provide efficient resource allocation. Techniques of appraisal have to be developed for goods and services provided by the state when the benefits cannot be measured in terms of the price which the user is prepared to pay. When collective goods are provided, such as defence, health services, roads and schools, without direct prices being charged for them, money values have to be imputed for the costs incurred and the benefits gained.

Where the price mechanism operates it is possible for a producer to make efficient investment decisions by comparing his payments with his receipts, thereby measuring the profitability of alternative investments. The problem in the public sector is to measure the benefits of investment in public goods which yield benefits to all, whether or not they pay for them, or where perhaps for political reasons there are no charges to users, as in the case of the police, clean air or the control of water pollution. Cost-benefit analysis is applicable where the state provides goods free of charge and recovers the costs through taxation, and where society pays for the effects of production not borne by the producer, such as air pollution from factories, noise from commercial aircraft or congestion from the geographical concentration of industry. 'The immediate distinction between a cost-benefit appraisal of expenditure policies and an appraisal in terms of private returns is, therefore, that CBA attempts to allow for all the gains and losses as viewed from the standpoint of society.'[5]

Imputing monetary values to the benefits of a project involves calculating where possible the consumers' surplus in addition to any market values. Alternatively shadow prices may have to be calculated for proposed new goods or services based on consumer behaviour in relation to alternative existing goods and services. Where monetary values are impossible to ascribe to a project's effect, other measures must be developed to provide a full picture of the consequences of given actions, and to permit comparison and judgement. Measuring noise in decibels is an example. Where no objective measure is possible, subjective rankings may be offered. In this way intangibles are openly recognised as such. Finally, the opportunity costs of the resources used must be calculated and included in the analysis.

Road developments, such as a motorway, provide good examples of these costing methods (and of the technical problems associated with them; see below). If a motorway reduces the price per vehicle mile by reducing operating costs and travelling time, a consumers' surplus is generated for those who maintain the same level of use, and for those who are attracted by the reduced costs. The problem of valuing time savings, both for work and leisure, introduces the notion of shadow prices. The land needed for a motorway has an opportunity cost equal to the value of its best alternative use. The problem of intangibles occurs when attempts are made to include the 'costs' of reduced amenity or the benefits of reduced congestion, such as less mental and physical strain on drivers and passengers.[6]

Time

Finally, there is the fact that costs and benefits accrue over time. Allowance has to be made for the different ways in which change in the future can affect the analyst's calculations.

The effects on the calculations of differential inflation must be predicted. This is where changes in the market prices of costs and benefits take place at different rates, such as wage increases relative to the prices of manufactured goods and raw materials. The prices of goods may also vary because of changes in the levels of supply or demand.

Then the political system has to decide how society values future benefits, compared with present ones which have to be forgone, by arriving at a social time preference discount rate. Finally, it is necessary to calculate the productivity lost in the public or private sectors as a consequence of investment in a specific project. Ways have to be selected of measuring the social opportunity costs of funds withdrawn for alternative forms of productivity.[7]

Uncertainty about the future may lead cost-benefit analysts to build a range of values into their calculations, such as different rates of discount. These indicate the objective probabilities of different outcomes where such probabilities can be assigned. Alternatively they assign subjective probabilities where there is no basis for enumerating the risks involved in achieving the predicted benefits and costs. Statistical analysis and computer models permit elaborate variations of values to be incorporated into the analysis.

Operations research contributes to problem-solving here by sensitivity analysis of forecasts which almost always involve some degree of error, especially where major investment projects can take many years to complete, such as motorways or underground rail links. Sensitivity analysis is carried out when the final outcome of a policy is highly sensitive to the probability of error in one of the predictions made about possible effects. The range of expectations for an assumption can be traced throughout the calculations and its effects on the final result measured. Risk analysis is a more elaborate technique in which sensitivity to a number of assumptions is measured simultaneously. The range of expectations is estimated for every assumption made about the future, and the effects of variations in predictions about numerous contributory factors are tested in combination.

For example, the planners of a city centre redevelopment scheme will have to predict the likely need for retail floor space on completion of the project, say ten years ahead. This prediction will be based on estimations of growth in annual spending per head of population, the growth in population, the percentage of spending in city centre shops, and the ratio of turnover to retail floor space. If there is a range of values for each prediction the final answer could reasonably vary greatly – in the case of one Coventry plan, for example, from 25 per cent less than allowed for by existing plans to 37 per cent more.[8]

An important question here is how 'reasonable' are the potential variations. Large elements of subjectivity may be involved, according to the type of uncertainty involved. It may be uncertainty about the specific socio-economic environment of the policy area, such as estimates of retail spending per head for urban redevelopment schemes or the prediction of traffic flows for road schemes. There may be even greater uncertainty about values, such as the required ratio of turnover to retail floor space required, or views on the relative desirability of safety, reduced congestion or construction costs on roads. Another source of uncertainty is the effect of decisions taken in related policy areas. Decisions about environmental control will have consequences for road developments, which in turn have implications for the allocation of retail spending between city centre and other shops. Operations research contributes in this last area of uncertainty with the analysis of interconnected decision areas which is being widely applied to government agencies in such diverse areas as town planning and the management structure of the Civil Service Department.[9]

Predictions of the future also affect present choices of action by revealing the flexibility of specified commitments. Operations research has developed 'robustness' criteria to show how many desired results may still be obtained if circumstances change in the future. 'Robust' decisions are those which leave the planner flexibility to achieve desired goals in the face of uncertainty.[10]

The investment criterion

When all the questions about the range and value of social and economic costs and benefits to be included in the analysis have been answered, it should in theory be possible to establish the benefit-cost ratios and net present values of different projects and so make an economically efficient choice. Calculation of the net present value of a project is possible when costs and benefits are measurable in monetary terms. Where there are non-monetary costs and benefits which can be quantified it will be necessary to itemise the incommensurable and intangible benefits and costs to allow for a rational appraisal of the projects being compared.[11] The investment criterion is based on a combination of highest net present value and the highest benefit-cost ratio and applied to the projects to choose the one with the greatest social profitability. It is a matter of political judgement how non-monetary costs and benefits should be weighted against monetary factors.

Political advantages

The political significance of cost-benefit analysis and related techniques should by now be pretty obvious. They give the appearance and often the reality of greater rationality to the process of policy-making. They enable policy-makers to reflect changing values and new conceptions of the public interest in policy-formation, such as the recognition of social costs and environmental externalities. Claiming hitherto unforeseen benefits may make it easier to win political support for a decision, such as recreational benefits from a river purification scheme or forestry. Finally, cost-benefit approaches present an opportunity to delegate decision-making to experts and so conveniently depoliticise the process.

This of course may backfire on the politicians, as happened in the case of locating a third international airport in the London region.

There are however many technical problems to be overcome before cost-benefit approaches can be used in policy-making with absolute confidence. These can best be outlined under three main headings: valuation, standardisation and distribution.

Valuation

There has consistently been great disagreement among the experts on the valuation in money terms of costs and benefits which cannot be valued through the expression of market preferences. Ascribing utilities to consumers under such circumstances can lead to arbitrary decisions being taken about the value of goods and services which will vary immensely according to income, wealth, the price of competing goods, location and time.

The valuation of human life and health has generated great controversy. Reductions in motor accidents, for example, can produce measurable savings by increasing industrial output and reducing medical expenses. But can money values be placed on personal suffering or sense of bereavement? Valuations of human life or disablement are made in the courts in cases of damages. Such awards are however not consistently made and cannot therefore provide an objective measure to the cost-benefit analyst. Life insurance values perhaps reflect the value of a person's life to his family, but not to himself. It is one thing to say that the value of a life should be based on the values of the person whose life is at risk, and of others from whom there are financial and psychic consequences. It is another thing to convert these values to monetary figures.

Many transportation projects, such as the location of a third London airport, have included the 'costing' of passenger time as an overwhelmingly important element in the cost-benefit calculations. Yet this has often involved relatively arbitrary valuations, especially in the case of leisure time saved by new road projects.

This is why 'the valuation of intangible benefits and costs presents perhaps the most serious problem in CBA, and the most controversial'.[12] Any assumption that surrogate or shadow prices are reflected in survey responses (about willingness to pay for saved time, for example), modal split (as in choices between alternative modes of travel) or changes in property values (as a result of noise, for example) is fraught with difficulties. When some non-monetary but quantitative measure of costs and benefits can be included in the analysis, such as increase or reduction in the crime rate, it may be possible to compare monetary values and intangibles. But most projects, if explored fully, will have more than one intangible, which raises the analytical problem of trading off, for example, noise against visual amenity.

Even where market prices exist for some goods or resources, they do not automatically reflect social costs. Imperfect competition and external effects, such as taxation, unemployment or balance of payments problems, operate to prevent market prices from reflecting the marginal costs which are usually accepted as society's valuation of some good or service. There are difficult practical and conceptual problems in correcting market prices to reflect marginal costs.[13]

Distribution

Project analysis based on market prices is sometimes criticised as perpetuating the present class bias of the economic system. Willingness to pay reflects ability to pay unless the differing marginal utilities of income are taken into account. Therefore projects which benefit higher income groups will appear more attractive in financial terms than those benefiting people on lower incomes. For example, the creation of working class amenities such as bingo halls and cinemas are likely to be weighted less than the destruction of middle class amenities, such as golf clubs and cultural monuments, when both are likely to be brought about by the siting of an international airport.

It has been suggested that cost-benefit studies should indicate the classes of people affected one way or another by the projects under review. Incorporating distributional weightings to alter income distribution between classes of people is, however, obstructed by many technical difficulties.[14] Equity considerations have to be left to the political rather than the economic system for resolution. Otherwise the consumer sovereignty implicit in cost-benefit analysis will perpetuate existing inequalities. In making public policy the politicians must decide 'whose utility function is to prevail'.[15]

Standardisation

Finally, there is the problem of standardising the techniques of cost-benefit analysis so that the different projects to which it might be applied are treated in the same way. Unfortunately there is as yet no set procedure for handling a cost-benefit appraisal of a public expenditure project. It is inevitable that the analysts responsible will take decisions based on their own values and judgements about such technicalities as the exact investment appraisal criterion or the rate of discount to be used. The boundaries of the exercise have also to be established. There are often many possible solutions to a problem which are not in fact included in cost-benefit studies. How is it decided which potential solutions should be excluded? Some alternatives are bound to be excluded before CBA begins. There is no way of preventing the inevitable sifting of solutions from excluding one which might be as good as another which is given the full CBA treatment. Again the judgement of the analyst is important.

Similar problems occur with the projects which are selected for comparison according to cost-benefit criteria. How can all its relevant effects be identified? Who is to say what effects are to count as relevant? If the effects of a motorway were to be fully explored all the important relationships between parts of the transportation system should be included. An ideal analysis would cover all possible combinations of different forms of transport and different policies of pricing, subsidy and control. This is a difficult and complex task. There is therefore the problem of designing the model or system of inputs and outputs so that all the relevant factors are included. But what the analyst thinks is important may exclude factors which others would wish to take into account. Transport economists, for example, tend to concentrate on factors amenable to certain analytical techniques, such as the transportation effects of completing a stretch of motorway, and the financial costs of construction. Social costs during construction and the effect on industrial location, employment, social life, and people without cars tend to be ignored. Problems are often in danger of being trivialised.

CASE STUDY: A RAIL LINK WITH HEATHROW AIRPORT

The best way to appreciate the use of cost-benefit analysis is to see it applied to a specific investment proposal. The example chosen here is the study of alternative rail links between central London and Heathrow Airport initiated in 1969 by the President of the Board of Trade and Minister of Transport.[16]

A link between central London and Heathrow had first been considered in 1956 but it was decided that there was insufficient traffic to justify the expenditure. Airline coach operations were made more viable by road improvements in the late 1950s and early 1960s, but by 1966 it again appeared that a rail link would be a reasonable financial proposition. Any such link would, however, have to operate in conjunction with the existing coach services since the airlines could not be expected to abandon them. These services also included check-in facilities in central London which could not be lost. Thus a rail link without this service, such as an underground line, would not suffice. In view of those constraints it was decided in 1969 to consider four alternative schemes:

1 An exclusive British Rail Link between Victoria and Heathrow, with check-in at Victoria and with coach services withdrawn;
2 A similar link to 1, but with coach services continuing;
3 A similar link to 2, but without check-in at Victoria;
4 Extension of the Piccadilly line to Heathrow, with coach services continuing.

All four schemes were compared with projections of the existing system of town terminals and coach operations, taking into account reductions in coach speeds resulting from the future growth of traffic congestion.

Estimates were made of the future growth in air passenger traffic only up to 1981 because of the uncertainty involved in longer range forecasts. Low and high estimates were made, based on cautious and optimistic views of increased runway capacity, the rate of growth in average aircraft size and the extent to which demand builds up in the less busy hours. The range of total traffic estimated for 1981 was from 31.5 to 42.2 million passengers a year. The expected 1981 passengers were classified by geographic area, and identified as business, leisure, resident or non-resident. Estimates were also made of airport staff and 'miscellaneous' traffic — people other than air passengers and airport staff travelling to and from the airport (e.g. spectators).

Predictions were made of future modal split under each of the proposed schemes on the basis of valuations of passenger business and leisure time, fares, vehicle operating costs and parking charges. In the absence of behavioural evidence to the contrary, comfort was assumed to be the same for all public links. The modal split figures were increased in line with estimates of staff needed for an air passenger flow of 30 million per year.

User costs were calculated on the direct money costs of the link to public transport users, plus users' time and comfort costs. Business time savings were costed on the basis of the average income of air travellers in 1968 and the expected increase in national average real wages. The problem of forecasting is well illustrated by the possibility for overestimation here: some business travellers may travel in their own time; much of the growth in air traffic may be from groups having lower incomes than today's passengers. This was most important to the Heathrow links study because of the higher proportion of business travellers than found in most modes of transportation. The values used had to be subjected to detailed sensitivity tests. Leisure time was then valued and in-town operating costs were calculated.

Two main categories of *indirect costs* were considered. One was crowding on the Piccadilly Line due to additional airport traffic particularly in the commuter peaks. This was considered as an unquantifiable factor because its effects could not be expressed in money terms on any generally agreed basis. The other was congestion costs experienced by road traffic due to the level of airport traffic on the roads. Time and cost savings were calculated for road users experiencing higher average journey speeds as a result of reductions in road miles travelled by airport passengers.

The *direct costs* of the different schemes included the construction costs of airline coaches and depot, rail rolling-stock, rail track, station platform, town and Heathrow terminals and road works. Staff costs were also included. A summary of all costs — user, indirect and direct — is given in Table 9.1 (based on high air traffic estimates). The numbers shown are the present values of discounted capital and annual costs from 1970—94. Negative figures represent cost savings (or benefits). The ratio of net benefits to outlay in the bottom line is the ratio of the sum of discounted annual cost changes over the additional capital cost, given a discount rate of 10 per cent.

The scheme involving an extension of the London Transport Piccadilly Line extension showed the highest total return on these calculations and the highest return per pound invested. The 'coach only' scheme had low capital but high annual operating costs. A further capital investment of £11.9 million (in present value terms) in the Piccadilly Line link indicated savings of £6.6 million in the value of operating costs for the reduced coach service then required. To break even on a cost-benefit basis required £5.3 million to be covered by additional benefits. All the other schemes left considerably more than this to be recouped.

TABLE 9.1
Cost-benefit summary (£000)

	Coaches only Cap.	Ann.	Scheme 1 Cap.	Ann.	Scheme 2 Cap.	Ann.	Scheme 3 Cap.	Ann.	Scheme 4 Cap.	Ann.
USER COSTS										
passengers	0	0		-19,364		-19,364		-35,365		-34,621
workers	0	0		0		0				-574
INDIRECT COSTS										
congestion		0		-926		-570		-880		-1,650
DIRECT COSTS										
link	765	18,281	15,119	6,842	14,769	14,777	14,065	13,359	11,388	10,423
terminals	417	7,298	8,598	13,764	8,185	15,048	3,126	8,487	2,323	8,604
road works	888		918		792		792		239	
TOTAL	2,070	25,579	24,635	316	23,746	9,891	17,983	-14,399	13,956	-17,818
LESS 'COACHES ONLY'	0	0	22,565	-25,263	21,676	-15,688	15,913	-39,978	11,886	-43,397
NET PRESENT VALUE				-2,698		5,988		-24,065		-31,511
RATIO OF NET BENEFITS TO OUTLAY				1.12		.73		2.50		3.65

Time savings, particularly business time, made up much the largest portion of the quantified benefits. The Piccadilly Line scheme came second to scheme 4 on this count, but this advantage was offset by the benefits to diverted traffic in savings of private resource costs achieved by the Piccadilly Line scheme.

Numerous assumptions had to be made before these results were arrived at, such as forecasts of future air traffic, values of business time and construction costs. Since variations in these assumptions could affect the comparisons it was necessary to carry out sensitivity tests to see the effects of the most extreme assumptions that seemed within the bounds of possibility. The best and worst specific assumptions for each scheme were tested. For example, the best assumptions made for the Piccadilly Line scheme were that there would be no comfort 'costs' for crowding, that direct costs would be reduced to the minimum, that the estimates of congestion cost saving would be maximised, and that the most favourable road cost-sharing formula (for new roadworks required by the schemes) would be adopted. The worst assumptions for this scheme included a notional charge on all passengers to represent relative lack of comfort, additions to direct costs to allow for contingencies such as new road works in connection with station developments and the least favourable road cost-sharing formula.

The result of the sensitivity testing was that the ranking of the schemes did not change on any reasonable combination of assumptions. On the best general assumptions the worst benefit-cost ratio for the Piccadilly scheme was better than the best for schemes 1 and 2. Under the worst general assumptions, the same conclusions were reached. Even on the worst possible combination of general and specific assumptions the benefits of the Piccadilly scheme were greater than its costs. The same applied to comparisons of scheme 3 with the Piccadilly link. The financial rates of return were sensitivity analysed with similar results.

The unquantifiable factors presented some characteristic problems to the group working on the Heathrow link. These had to be identified and examined to see whether the net differences between the schemes evaluated in terms of such factors indicated the same choices as the quantified elements. If different choices were indicated it would then be necessary to weigh the unquantified factors against the cost differences already set out.

Six factors were selected as significant and assessed for their effects

TABLE 9.2
Unquantified factors

Factors	1	2	3	4
Choice of two public modes	no	yes	yes	yes
Option of check-in in central London	yes	yes	no	no
Comfort	good	good	good	fair/good
Baggage handling	very good*	very good*	fair/good	fair
Reliability	good	good	good	very good
Town planning implications	acceptable	acceptable	acceptable	acceptable

*Assumes a reliable system can be developed.

on each scheme. Some were also tested by placing arbitrary money values on them.

Detailed assessments were made of the disadvantages of the Piccadilly Line in not offering full baggage handling facilities, not guaranteeing adequate seating capacity at all times and not offering a full twenty-four hour service. Note was taken of the numbers and sizes of bags carried by airline passengers and the fact that it is common for holiday-makers to carry their baggage on the Underground. In order to investigate standards of comfort the downward trend in commuter passenger traffic on the western sections of the Piccadilly Line was projected, with sensitivity tests, to 1981. Even with most pessimistic assumptions about peak-hour loadings it was found that there would be capacity, within London Transport's comfort standard, to carry all the estimated traffic on the Heathrow link. These calculations ignored the Underground's other advantages, such as reliability in adverse weather conditions and interconnection with other passenger transport services.

The analysis of the proposed British Rail links showed that while not increasing the consumer surplus by as much as the cheaper Piccadilly link, they offered better comfort and baggage handling.

The study group concluded that scheme 1 should be excluded because it was unlikely that the airlines would be prepared to withdraw their own coach services; the cost-benefit ratio was poor; its financial viability was doubtful; and it restricted choice. Its unquantified advantage was its potential for sophisticated baggage handling.

Scheme 2 offered good standards of comfort and convenience but ranked lowest in cost-benefit and financial terms. To make it comparable with scheme 3 the check-in facilities at Victoria had to be given an unreasonably high valuation. Scheme 3 offered a shorter journey than scheme 4 (the Piccadilly Line), better baggage facilities, and a guaranteed seat. These were the factors which finally had to be set against London Transport's cheaper fare, slight advantage in reliability and much better showing in terms of the cost-benefit analysis and returns on investment. In addition it provided dispersed access over central London and an added transport facility *within* the airport.

Having quantified costs and benefits wherever possible, compared unquantifiable factors and tested the effects of different assumptions, forecasts and values, the study group concluded:

> We do not believe that there is a credible set of assumptions which would make any of the other schemes preferable to the Piccadilly Line extension . . . There are considerable benefits to be gained by supplementing the present coach services between Central London and Heathrow by a rail link. If a rail link is built then it should be an extension of London Transport's Piccadilly Line from Hounslow West to Heathrow.[17]

The Heathrow Link Steering Group published its report in May 1970. Its recommendation proved to be politically viable. London Transport sought the Greater London Council's approval of the extension. GLC elections were due the following April, and an improvement of the Piccadilly Line was an obvious electoral asset. In July the GLC approved London Transport's plan to extend the Piccadilly Line to Hatton Cross and Heathrow. This was subject to the British Airports Authority agreeing to make a satisfactory contribution towards the cost and the government agreeing to meet 75 per cent of the cost of the three and a half mile extension.

However the Minister of Transport decided that the government could not contribute on the grounds that the extension would be able to pay its way. In November 1970 the GLC Policy and Resources Committee recommended that the Council should provide £3.7 million towards the cost of the £15 million extension, with the balance on loan to London Transport either from the Public Works Loan Board or from the Council itself. The committee also recommended that an all-party deputation should be sent to the Secretary of State for the Environment to discuss the government's decision.

The GLC gave authority for the project to be started, but in January 1971 the government again refused a grant towards the cost of the link.

In March the first contract was signed for civil engineering works between Hounslow West and Hatton Cross on the airport perimeter.

By September 1972 the capital costs had risen to £22.7 million. (It rose further to £27 million by July 1975). The government then agreed to pay a 25 per cent grant, leaving London Transport to find 50 per cent and the G LC 25 per cent. Stage one was completed in July 1975 with the opening of a new station at Hatton Cross and the completion of the whole project is due in 1977.

CONCLUSION

The analysis of the costs and benefits of alternative ways of solving a problem reveals difficulties which exemplify the limitations on pure rationality of which policy-makers must always be aware. Yet there is no question that such calculations ought to form part of the policy-making process. It may be that ultimately economic considerations are out-weighed by political factors. This is not to imply that elaborate and expensive research to determine the former is always a waste of time. 'An important advantage of a cost-benefit study is that it forces those responsible to quantify cost and benefits as far as possible rather than rest content with vague qualitative judgements or personal hunches.'[18] If politicians go against the recommendations of economists they should at least know the price to the community of taking such action. The fact that techniques of project appraisal have not yet developed to produce complete and certain forecasts of future costs and benefits does not mean that it is not worth knowing what can be predicted with some degree of confidence.

CHAPTER 10

Information

All large organisations, especially governments, experience information problems when planning policies. The more sophisticated decision-making becomes, the greater is the need for high quality information. This applies to all stages of the policy-making process. Information is needed for understanding the nature and magnitude of social and economic problems. It is essential to the selection of alternative methods of solving them. It is crucial in assessing the consequences of chosen policy instruments for the problems at which they are directed. 'A policy-maker without information on the quantitative consequences of his policies is in the position of a businessman who doesn't know the value of his sales.'[1]

THE NEED FOR INFORMATION

That there exists in British government a need for such information, especially on the consequences of public policy, is obvious. That it is lacking is also becoming increasingly obvious. The House of Commons Expenditure Committee recently concluded that: 'The system of information necessary for resource accountability does not at present exist; this means that neither the Government, nor Parliament nor the public can at present be supplied with the material necessary for any systematic discussion or evaluation of priorities.'[2] The Treasury has also admitted that adequate information on the outputs of public expenditure programmes — measurements of what has been obtained for money spent — has not been available to policy-makers.[3] Government departments, including the Treasury, have relied more on the judgement or 'feel' of their divisions and subordinate agencies than on any system of hard information. In the absence of adequate informa-

160

tion systems it is impossible to determine the effectiveness of expenditure by verifying that services have been improved in some quantifiable sense or that the environment has been changed in some desired direction.

For example, although a number of policies have been devised to meet the needs of the elderly, the information relevant to evaluating them is derived from observations of the services or institutions provided and not the users or clients of those services. Objectives are defined in very general terms, such as 'to enable the elderly to maintain their independence and self-respect' or 'to provide treatment and care of an appropriate standard for those suffering from chronic disabilities'. There is no information available to define these objectives in precise, measurable terms, thus enabling policy-makers to calculate how far they have been reached and whether achievements can be ascribed to the health and personal social services or to other factors. Consequently officials of the Department of Health and Social Security 'do not know how much they spend on the elderly, and they are at a very early stage in working towards a complete information system'.[4] Without the expression of objectives in quantifiable terms, little can be done in monitoring progress.

The case of nursery education also illustrates these problems. This has both educational and social objectives; but it is not known how many children 'need' nursery education, nor what the demand would be if it were provided free universally but not compulsorily. The emphasis on resources rather than output can also lead to the situation where a notably progressive education authority, such as Sheffield, can discover that despite its modern educational system a high proportion of children have unexpected visual, oral or neurological handicaps, are poorly motivated educationally and are generally less happy than five years ago. Educational planners have paid too little attention to the non-educational factors affecting their objectives, such as family stress and breakdown, rehousing problems, worry about employment prospects, or even the fact that unskilled jobs commanded relatively high rates of pay. They basically know nothing about the causes of unhappiness and under-achievement.[5] Survey material has been produced which confirms impressions of this kind. People have expressed their lowest levels of satisfaction for areas of life, such as leisure, housing and education, in which there have been considerable advances in terms of inputs in recent years, measured by expenditure on leisure, houses built and numbers in higher education.[6]

Information problems in government occur at all stages of the policy process, from the appraisal of problems, through the prediction of the results from possible lines of action, to the evaluation of the effects of chosen policies on the original problem. Since most perceived problems are already under the influence of some existing policy, it is possible to conclude that there is a great need for what might be termed 'output' information as distinct from 'input' information, or information about the resource costs of policies: in other words, information about the environment and what the relationships are between changes in the environment and changes in public policy. It is in this area, rather than in the costing of policies, that information gaps are becoming increasingly apparent in British government. As the Expenditure Committee put it recently:

> The idea of a comprehensive set of statistics of outputs over the whole range of public expenditure is an ambitious one. But we believe that it ought to be regarded as a realistic and reasonable aim. Patient work by the Civil Service and computer techniques have given us, through measurement of expenditure at constant prices, one of the most sophisticated analyses of inputs in the world; we think that the possibilities inherent in the present system will not be fully realised until the analysis of inputs is matched by an analysis of outputs.[7]

A major effort is being made to quantify the environment by the development of social indicators which are comparable to the economic indicators which provide measures of the national income and production. While national income statistics indicate economic welfare in aggregate terms they reveal little about the quality of social life. First, they do not measure the 'externalities' which are not reflected in the market price of goods and services, such as the costs of pollution, urban congestion, crime and illness, or the benefits of scientific research, education, stable family life or cultural development. Secondly, they present a misleading picture of welfare by including in the national income expenditure on things which society may well wish to avoid, such as restoring assets affected by the many different kinds of pollution.

It is precisely such costs and benefits that governments, rather than individuals, must act upon. As private individuals, 'we have no incentive to curtail those activities that bring losses to others, but no cost to ourselves'.[8] Such activities produce problems which are said to be related to the public interest and which can only usually be dealt with by collective action.

Hence the social indicators 'movement' which seeks to augment the information which is available about the expenditures and activities of governments and about the economy, which is well-developed, with information about the problems which governments sometimes attempt to solve (or which we may feel they ought to try to solve) and the extent to which they are being successful. What has been said with reference to the USA seems equally applicable to Britain: 'We need information about the condition of our society; about how much children have learned, not about the time and money used for schooling; about health, not about the number of licensed doctors; about crime, not about the number of policemen; about pollution, not about the agencies that deal with it.'[9] In the case of health, for example, it is necessary to distinguish measures of output from measures of environmental conditions and health service provision, both of which are measures of input. Indicators of environmental factors, such as the quality of the water supply, provide no information of the state of a community's health. Neither do such indicators as the numbers of hospital beds, patients admitted and treated, or doctors per thousand of population: 'Indicators of State-of-Health need to be quite free of any input content in order that the effects on them of varying input combinations may be subsequently estimated.'[10] Eventually the aim is to integrate social data into an information system comparable to the national accounts.[11]

This goal is a long way off, but considerable progress has been made towards it. The Government Social Survey, the Central Statistical Office and the social policy departments have greatly improved the quantity and quality of information available. There is now quite a wide range of significant statistical series related to social policies and conditions. Once the descriptive data has been built up it will be the task of those concerned with social indicators to derive from them new measures of the state of society and the quality of life. Statistical data will become the components of indices which will have an evaluative function and which will measure how far different sectors of society are well-fed, healthy, living a full life-span, well-housed, enjoying job-satisfaction, receiving sufficient education, living in physical security, and even enjoying personal liberty and justice.[12] Social indicators assume the collection of data specifically for policy-formation.

The demand in public organisations for more and improved

information in policy-analysis is usually accompanied by demands for changes in organisational structures. This is nothing new. It can be traced back at least as far as the Haldane Report of 1918 and reappears in the Fulton Report of 1968.[13] The latter recommended that each government department should allocate responsibility for policy-planning to a planning and research unit headed by a senior policy adviser with direct access to the minister. As the need for research and information has grown, either within individual departments or for the government as a whole, organisational changes have been made by establishing planning units alongside managerial hierarchies, or by setting up analytical capabilities to serve the Cabinet, as in the case of the Central Policy Review Staff for strategic planning in central government.

Usually such units consist of multi-professional or multi-disciplinary teams organised in flexible, collegiate rather than hierarchical structures. The CPRS, for example, is a small, multi-disciplinary group of scientists and economists drawn from the civil service, business, the universities and international organisations. It was set up in 1971 to assist ministers collectively in making policy choices and establishing priorities by ensuring that 'the underlying implications of alternative courses of action are fully analysed and considered'.[14] It has cultivated the image of an intellectual 'think tank' with very informal, non-hierarchical procedures and structure. Its work has fallen into two main categories: advice on priorities between policies within the government's overall strategy; and advice on the most efficient means of reaching stated objectives.[15]

Most central departments now have planning units, branches or directorates. They are all relatively small and staffed by career civil servants drawn from both the generalist and specialist groups. The specialists are usually economists or statisticians, although there are scientists in some Ministry of Defence research units and doctors in DHSS. In addition to units charged with policy-analysis most departments have specialist divisions and research branches providing professional supporting services and information relevant to policy development, such as the Home Office Research Unit.[16]

In local government the growing interest in policy-planning within a corporate and community framework has also generated demands for new organisational structures to feed information and analysis into the policy-making process at both official and political levels. So far most local authorities still rely on the functional departments to provide committees of officers and councillors with information. However the virtues of specialised planning units are increasingly being recognised. Local authorities have set up interdisciplinary teams to gather information and provide a wider range of policy choices to both officials and politicians.[17]

None of these developments obscure the fact that policy-planners in British government are some way from acquiring information which would enable them to complete the policy-making cycle. Indeed, there will always be new information to acquire as social and economic conditions change. It is important to develop information systems by which planners can 'top up' their reserves of information as not only conditions but political values change. This is easier said than done. What obstacles stand in the way of establishing this necessary condition of rationality? They are associated with the creation of information — with gathering, processing and interpreting data; and with its communication.

INFORMATION PROBLEMS

Costs

The first problem, which relates specifically to the gathering and processing of new data, is that it can make heavy demands on scarce resources. The British Treasury, in replying to the suggestion that information should be provided which would show whether expenditure had achieved the standard of service provision planned, stated that: 'The fundamental difficulty now is the sheer volume of detailed but highly skilled work that is needed to achieve results by specialist staff with many other calls on their time.'[18] The cost-effectiveness of information gathering must never be overlooked, especially when a government can arrive in the position in which the US federal government found itself in 1967. A Congressional committee revealed that more than 5,000 forms were approved by the Bureau of the Budget which were estimated to take almost 110 million man-hours to complete. At the same time the federal government employed nearly 19,000 statistical workers and spent $888 million on automatic data processing, computer equipment and statistical studies under contract to private firms.

It is also costly in terms of time. So often decisions have to be taken before information can be gathered. The Department of Health and Social Security, for example, could develop indices of social mobility and other indicators of the health and social well-being of the elderly in order to measure the extent to which their general objectives are being achieved, 'but it would take many years to establish a complete information system relating to needs assessed in these terms'.[19] In the meantime health services have to be planned and run, and many irreversible decisions will be taken. The Social Malaise Study carried out in Liverpool during 1968—9 illustrates this problem further.

> Whilst it was underway, community development and allied activities also progressed. Thus on completion of the Malaise work ... it has not functioned in quite the way envisaged ... In fact because community development and movements in planning theory and practice are so rapid, it is impossible to devise a context within which to draw up a once-and-for-all comprehensive community development programme, still less to base such a programme on one piece of research.[20]

It should perhaps come as no surprise to find impatience among administrators who are asked by planners for more and more information. Local authorities in particular become extremely irritable when required by central departments to provide statistics which are expensive in terms of staff and delays in completing other work, and which often seem of little value to the authority which has to collect them.[21] When finance is short, too, information is vulnerable, as shown by the 1975 Budget decision to abandon the five-yearly sample census.

On a more theoretical level, there is another scarce resource: man's intellectual ability. This is one of the weaknesses of the rational model of decision-making and planning. It not only assumes that 'complete' information could be acquired. It also assumes that it could be comprehended and incorporated into the planning framework. 'To the extent that information becomes complete, it imposes increasingly severe strains on man's cognitive faculties.'[22] The fact that complete information cannot be acquired nor comprehended has led planners to narrow their focus and isolate their problem area from irrelevant connections. The planner thus selects what he believes to be the relevant factors connected with the decision which he has to make — what Simon calls a 'closed system of variables'.[23] Thus the choice between alternative strategies which is so central to policy-making is not only determined by the actual relationships between variables. It is also conditioned by the initial choice of variables to be related. For example, one planner might attempt to measure the effect of public expenditure on a problem, such as housing provision, while another might include in the analysis the effects of 'tax expenditure', that is the exclusions, exemptions and preferential rates that might be available, such as tax deductions for interest paid on home mortgages. Hence the planner's values, as well as his analytical capabilities, affect the gathering of information.

Values

A second problem is that individual, administrative and political interests can influence the collection and interpretation of data. The official, for example, may 'screen out' information which adversely affects his interests or the interests of his department. Bias may intrude in order to find easy solutions, obtain consensus or avoid uncertainty.[24] In a recent study of expenditure planning in British government it was found that departments, in deciding which policies should be subject to programme analysis and review, were heavily influenced by what was politically convenient and what they knew would provide arguments for increasing their levels of spending.[25] The fear of official bias in the search for new information for policy-making has led some ministers to bring their own 'trusted' advisers into Whitehall on taking office — the Whitehall 'irregulars'.

The collection and interpretation of new data is by no means a neutral exercise. The planner's own theories and values will be brought to bear in the evaluation of information. Decisions will be as much influenced by these theories and values as by new information.[26] It may, for example be felt that what can be measured and counted should be given more weight than the immeasurable or uncountable, on the grounds that the former is more rational. The latter may be damagingly neglected or undervalued, as in some cost-benefit studies. Values also influence the collection of data — a representative sample of adult opinions, for example, presupposes the equality of value of those opinions.[27]

Specialisation on the basis of skills, procedures or knowledge which is found in government also affects the planner's perceptions of problems and solutions. Different experts will view problems differently, according to the techniques of analysis and manipulation with which they are familiar. For example, autism and subnormality were

once defined exclusively as medical problems. Since the involvement of
other experts more successful results have been achieved by their
treatment as educational and social problems. There may also be
disagreement within a professional group. Members of the medical
profession often disagree about treatment and therefore official policy:
'No sooner has one committee of eminent doctors recommended that
all births should take place in hospital – and the recommendation
accepted – than another eminent specialist points out that there is no
evidence that this will cut down mortality.'[28] The knowledge of the
expert is thus never completely objective.[29]

Information in policy-making is sought and collected in order to
answer questions relating to specific problems. Often these questions,
far from being phrased in a purely objective way, are constructed under
the powerful influence of political values. The information collected
and the answers produced thus reflect the values which conditioned the
original question.

The following lists of questions, designed to show the choices before
the electorate in 1974, reveal how questions can be constructed so as to
extract answers that are favourable to an established predisposition.
The first list is taken from a *Times* leader of 6 February 1974. The
second is from a letter from Mr J. Petrie of Exeter University, objecting
to *The Times's* questions which, in his view, elicited answers favourable
to the Conservative government, and offering 'an alternative list,
containing the same questions but reconstructed so as to encourage the
opposite result'.

The importance of 'problem definition' is further illustrated by the
case of the 1968 Royal Commission on Medical Education. The
Commission defined the problem as deciding how many doctors were
needed. It did not define the problem as deciding which services were
required by the community. Consequently it ignored the contribution
to health care of non-medical skills and services. 'In short, the way the
Royal Commission defined the problem largely determined its policy
recommendations.'[30]

Information itself may be a powerful political weapon if it throws
light on a problem which hitherto has attracted little attention because
it could not be perceived clearly. 'It has often been observed that
nations rarely become effectively concerned with problems until they
learn to measure them.'[31] Groups vary in the resources at their disposal
for 'advertising' their problems and their claims on resources. Information, such as that 85 per cent of tax-payers are prepared to be worse off

TABLE 10.1

The Times's list	*Mr Petrie's list*
Should the Government give the miners what they want?	Should the Government give the miners what they believe they justly deserve?
Should the NUM be allowed to overrule an elected Government?	Should an elected government be allowed to appease its supporters by coercing its opponents?
Is conciliation and concession a better way to deal with trade union demands than resistance and firmness?	Is conciliation and firmness a better way to deal with trade union demands than resistance and concession?
Should we have wage and price controls to tackle inflation, or will price controls alone do the job?	Are price controls necessary for tackling inflation or are wage controls sufficient?
Who can best handle the dangerous economic situation that exists in 1974, including problems of the future of sterling?	Does the Government's recent record suggest that it can well handle the dangerous economic situation that exists in 1974, including problems of the future of sterling?
Which has been the better record, that of the Wilson administration of 1964—70, or the Heath administration of 1970—74?	Which has the worse record, the Wilson administration of 1964—70 or the Heath administration of 1970—74?
Was the policy of British entry into the EEC right?	Was the policy of British entry into the EEC wrong?
Was Britain right in her relatively pro-Arab stance of recent years, or should we have followed Mr Wilson's line of stronger support for Israel?	Was the Government right in its relatively pro-Arab stance of recent years or should it have followed the public desire for support for Israel?
Should there be a major extension of state ownership?	Should there be an extension of public participation in economic affairs?
Which party will be more successful in rapid development of the North Sea?	Which party is more likely to ensure British, rather than multi-national company, control over North Sea resources?
Which party has greater unity in a critical period?	Which party is more likely to allow internal freedom of discussion, vital at a critical period?

if the money was spent on raising pensions, or that modernisation and not new building increases the number of homes, may alter the priority which society gives to a particular problem. This does not mean, of course, that values can be 'proved' by facts. The fairness of comprehensive education, for example, cannot be 'proved' by facts about the performance of comprehensive schools. Such information, however, can first demonstrate the value of comprehensive schools in terms which even their opponents appreciate, such as their examination records, and secondly reveal that the opponents are not really interested in fairness but in privilege. Information clears the ground so that conflicts of values are revealed for what they are.

Quantification

A third problem is that much of the new information required in policy-making involves devising quantitative measures of qualitative values. How can the components of a good and happy life be measured? How can we measure a congenial environment, work satisfaction or even health? It may be argued that the quality of life in a community depends heavily upon the extent of social integration, citizen participation, community concern and racial equality. But would it be agreed that these values can be measured by the number of drug addicts per thousand population, voting turnout, contributions per head to charity and unemployment rates?[32] The fact that such questions are difficult to answer is not to be explained simply by an absence of data or relevant research. It is to be explained by the fact that different people value different things. They consequently disagree about how they would value more or less of some quality and, therefore, how they would use it as a measure of success or failure in the pursuit of some policy objective. For example, there may be considerable agreement that the benefits of reduced overcrowding in prisons can be measured by number of reconvictions, disciplinary reports, disturbances, prisoners reporting sick for trivial reasons and escapes (presumably prisoners would not agree with the last item as a measure of benefit, unless the rate increased).[33] There is, however, much less agreement about the numerical values to be attached to amenities and ancient monuments when a site for an international airport has to be found. Or we might question how the life of a soldier comes to be valued at 1 per cent of a wealthy civilian's.[34] The examples illustrate the advantage which economics has over sociology: it has a measure of account, (money) and a theoretical framework which allows the interrelationships between many forms of economic activity to be specified.[35]

Even here, however, the need to consider such weightings is a pressure towards the clarification of objectives. For the value which planners and politicians attach to, say, reading ability as against economic returns in the case of indicators of performance in education will depend very much on what they regard as education's purpose.

Even if it were possible to agree on some overall measure of health, education or housing, the problem of aggregating them into a measure of welfare cannot be solved by more information. It is extremely valuable to know what effect an extra nursery school or old people's home has on a community, but only judgement and values enable us to decide which we prefer. It is extremely important in government that policy-makers should know where ethical and political judgements take over from data collection and analysis. This is where the social indicator 'accounts' fall short of the National Income Accounts.[36]

Cause and effect

There is also the statistical problem of identifying cause and effect between input variables, in terms of public expenditure, types of service and standards of administration, and output variables measured in terms of changes in the environment or in the circumstances of client groups. Research into recidivism among offenders, for example, has revealed how difficult it is to identify causal influences. In the evaluation of public policy generally it is difficult to isolate the influences which stem from governmental action from those which are outside the control of the authorities. To take the case of recidivism again, a great deal of what happens to ex-prisoners depends on factors not under the control of the Home Office, such as the economic conditions in the parts of the country to which ex-prisoners go to seek employment.[37]

Communication

Finally, information has to be communicated. No single individual can produce all the information needed in policy-making. The contributions of different specialists have to be integrated. In administrative organisations structures have to be devised to facilitate communication. It is by no means easy to decide which structure is appropriate to the type of communication required in policy-making.

There is some evidence to suggest that certain types of problem-solving require group interaction rather than individuals working on problems in isolation. Groups introduce a competitive spirit which mobilises intellectual energy. Social interaction in groups provides an error-correcting mechanism through which ideas are sifted. Collaboration in a group effort provides social support and approval which also facilitate problem-solving. Consequently when the essential task is one of finding the best solution to a problem among several alternatives the different frames of reference that individuals bring to a group help in the search.[38]

If such group communication is relevant to the type of problem-solving found in policy-making organisations it is important that structural features do not damage it. Hierarchy, involving a differentiation of status, may impede group processes in a number of ways. Explicit status distinctions may damage social interaction and social support. Formal status differences may undermine the process of competition for respect and therefore the group's problem-solving capacity. Status differences may also distort the error-correcting function of social interaction by encouraging deference and discouraging criticism.

Sociological and psychological findings such as these strongly suggest that egalitarian structures are better for policy-making. However hierarchy may not be totally dysfunctional. Indeed it may serve to ease communication and problem-solving in precisely those situations which so often occur in governmental decision-making.

First, an element of hierarchy and leadership may remove obstacles to communication and so improve a group's problem-solving ability when conflicting interests are at stake. The function of leadership here is to ensure that a dominant element in the group does not block the contribution of information by minority elements. The role of committee chairman is a case of such leadership.

Secondly, policy-planners not only solve problems. They have to establish a consensus. Experiments have shown that hierarchical differentiation may facilitate the coordination required for arriving at an agreed solution, rather than at the absolutely best solution. So far as a single correct or best solution is required, hierarchy and status differentiation may impede communication; so far as efficient coordination is required, hierarchically differentiated groups may be superior to undifferentiated groups.[39]

The problem of organisational choice for policy-planning is therefore a very difficult one. The solution to it may vary with the stage of the planning process reached. If alternative solutions are being sought, the undifferentiated group may be better than a group with hierarchy. When, however, the stage of choosing one of the alternatives and securing some consensus on the choice has been reached, an element of hierarchy may be beneficial. A flexible organisational structure would seem to be demanded by the information needs of policy-planning.

There are many other organisational problems which might be considered, such as finding the right relationship between planners and executive branches in government departments. These cannot be pursued further here since they would draw us too far from the purpose of this book. The organisation of planning generally, as well as the collection and communication of information, is something which deserves full and separate treatment.

PART IV

CHAPTER 11

Pluralism, Elitism and the Ruling Class

The object of this concluding chapter is to examine the power structure of the British state. It broadens the perspective of the book by moving beyond the process of policy-making in government to consider some elements of the socio-economic structure which are relevant to the way in which power is exercised in society generally.

This is a difficult task because of the disagreement among political scientists over the appropriate conceptual schemes to be used in the analysis of community power. Such disagreement is usually caused by ideological differences. Indeed ideological presuppositions have often led political scientists to take a theory of the state for granted and thereby neglect power and the state as a focus for political analysis.[1] Also the structure of power relationships is a subject that has been treated systematically by political scientists mainly with reference to local communities and city government, rather than to the nation state. Finally, all approaches to community power encounter serious methodological problems which cannot be adequately dealt with here but which will be alluded to throughout this chapter.

Most studies of British politics, so far as they concern themselves with the power structure of the state, accept either explicitly or implicitly one or other of the two models of community power which predominate in this area of political science: pluralism or class elitism.

PLURALISM

The pluralistic model corresponds closely to the theory of legitimate power set out in Chapter 3 above. It has a number of interrelated elements each of which corresponds to aspects of the British political system.

First, political equality and individualism are protected by the fundamental political rights to vote, to free speech and to association for political ends. Inequalities may, as was shown in Chapter 4, result from the operation of the electoral system, but these are random in their effects and do not favour any one socio-economic group. Representative institutions and the rights of opposition protect individual and sectional interests from unfair or arbitrary discrimination. The narrow electoral margins which have separated the two main political parties since the war have contributed to the maintenance of a balance between social and economic interests. Access to government is guaranteed through electoral choice, through lobbying and other forms of pressure group activity and through the politically free mass media.

Secondly, the weakness of the individual citizen in a modern democracy is compensated for by the right and ability of all freely to organise groups and associations for political action. Interests can be mobilised and made politically effective by the processes of functional representation. In a pluralist society power is diffused between such groups. Their rough equality of power produces a balanced competition for resources leading to democratic policy-making. Equilibrium is maintained by the countervailing power of different groups with different power-bases. Chapter 4 examined the relative power position of different groups in different political situations.

Thirdly, the state in a pluralist society is regarded as a neutral set of institutions for adjudicating between conflicting social and economic interests. The positive state is thought to protect all economic interests by accommodating and reconciling them. It does not defend the predominance of any particular class or show any marked bias towards a particular interest. No organisation or interest is consistently successful in obtaining its objectives across the whole range of public policies, and policy issues tend to be resolved in ways generally compatible with the preferences of the majority of the public.[2] The pre-war power of the capitalist class over economic matters has been whittled down by a transference of economic power to the state itself and to the trade union movement, through fiscal policies, physical controls over industry, nationalisation and the effects of full employment.[3]

Fourthly, although every state has its elites, including a political elite, the pluralist state is characterised by a plurality of elites. The nature of mass democracy and large-scale organisations may be such that power is inevitably concentrated in the hands of political leaders rather than the mass electorate or rank-and-file members of political organisations. This phenomenon was explained in relation to British government in Chapters 5 & 6. Nevertheless this is compatible with democracy if positions within the elites are open to people recruited from diverse socio-economic backgrounds. Pluralism can exist when no single elite dominates the political system and when access to elite positions is based on merit. Competition for power between elites simply refines the competition between interests by recognising the inevitabilities of organisational life. Competition between the political parties is further evidence of elite plurality.[4] Furthermore it is maintained that in Britain the different economic, social, political, professional, administrative and other elites lack the cohesion necessary to turn them into a ruling class.

In Britain pluralism is manifested in the decline of class and ideological politics and the rise of organised producer and consumer groups as the main channels of political communication between the people and the government. The pluralist character of British politics, and the relationships between groups and parties, has been most elaborately documented by Samuel Beer. He concluded that in the post-war period the Conservative and Labour Parties moved away from their more ideological standpoints and class antagonisms towards a consensus based on acceptance of the welfare state and the managed economy. Their attitudes towards policy-making in these areas may still be conditioned by contrasting values about equality and political authority. Nevertheless party conflict and group pressures operate within a broad consensus of 'collectivist' values and beliefs which 'legitimated party government by two purposive, strongly united and elaborately organized parties — along with functional representation by similarly concentrated producer's organizations'.[5]

Finally, the picture which emerges from the discussion in Part III of the techniques of policy-analysis in British government is also compatible with the pluralist conception of decision-making in democratic government. 'Bounded rationality' leads to incremental and marginal adjustments to existing goals and policies. The intellectual difficulties impeding rational behaviour fit neatly into the pluralists' model of politics as a process in which group competition within a broad consensus of goals serves to make marginal adjustments to the *status quo*. Consequently the organisational and political requirements of comprehensive, synoptic planning are rejected in favour of decentralised and dispersed decision-making powers: 'A spontaneous form of partisan mutual adjustment (PMA) among the various decision actors or centres is much to be preferred to the vain (but perhaps vainglorious) intellectual labours of central planners.'[6] 'Partisan mutual adjustment' is virtually another label for the pluralist political system in which consensus is maintained by a process of 'successive limited comparisons' in policy-making. 'Agreement on policy thus becomes the only practicable test of the policy's correctness.'[7]

CLASS ELITISM

How comprehensive is the pluralist model as an explanation of the British power structure? Several methodological problems are revealed by pluralist theory as well as some additional evidence of the distribution of power in British society and politics which make it necessary to take the analysis further. The term 'class elitism' has been chosen to sum up the factors about to be considered because it denotes the idea of the political elite being open only to members of the dominant economic class within a capitalist society and acting so as to protect the privileged position of that class. Class elitism refers to the political system of a society in which there is a 'ruling class' in the sense of an economically dominant and cohesive social group which owns the major instruments of economic production and controls the political instruments of resource allocation. How far are there elements of such a system in the British state?

Equality of power

First, British politics are not characterised by equally powerful group interests as is required by the pluralist model. Certainly many groups advocate and engage in political action according to what Trevor Smith has called the 'stiletto heel' principle, 'that if you put all your weight on one place you can go through almost anything'.[8] Party politics is denigrated as reflecting outmoded class divisions and redundant ideologies. But this in itself benefits the economically dominant middle class in two ways.

One is that the articulation of interests by extensive recourse to group activity and direct action at the expense of the aggregation of interests weakens the party system and impedes the operation of democratic politics. Only parties can determine the priorities to be allocated among the numerous 'one-off' solutions pressed upon governments by organised interests. Only parties, that is, can define the public interest and represent the national constituency. The anti-party, pluralist movement enables a government to divide and rule, or to avoid ruling at all. Either way radical solutions are easily contained: 'The proliferation of causes by means of direct action and militant lobbying can be very counter productive.'[9] The consensus sought by the balance of particular interests is almost certainly to be that of the middle class.

The other way that the middle class benefits from a pluralist strategy is through the inequalities of power between different groups. The classic pluralist fallacy is that all groups have equal resources. Producer groups are more powerful than consumer groups. Sectional interests are generally more powerful than promotional interests. Some 'interests' are poorly organised or not organised at all. As regards that most fundamental conflict, between capital and labour, it is the former which enjoys a strategic position in its dealings with government by virtue of its control of economic resources. The lack of influence which labour has over economic decision making in capitalist enterprises is carried over into its relations with the state. Labour has no foreign support, its determination to use industrial action is vulnerable, its leadership is less representative of the rank and file than is the case with business organisations, and it is more divided internally than business interests.

Labour leaders have less access to senior politicians and officials in the administration than business leaders, simply because the latter share a social and educational background and a common set of ideological values with the members of the state elite. This common ideology means that businessmen tend to be trusted in governing circles more than other spokesmen. There is 'a spiritual *rapport* even before contact is made on a particular issue'.[10] The close connections between the political authorities and private capital gives the latter great advantages when it comes to access.

Labour's demands are always more easily represented as more sectional than those of business which have more success in political circles in presenting their demands as serving the 'national interest'. More important, business interests can act to promote their own conceptions of the public interest by refusing to cooperate with the state in the formulation and implementation of commercial and industrial policies of which they do not approve.

Finally, business can bring more resources to bear on government agencies. It can raise money and sustain expenditure on propaganda, support to party funds and lobbying to a far greater extent than other interest groups.

Another defect of pluralist theory which encourages assumptions about the dispersal and equality of power is that it concentrates on political decisions and government policies, and ignores the power which economic domination confers outside the areas of state activity. Concentrated economic power and wealth in the hands of a minority inevitably expands the area of personal choice in terms of life style and standard of living of that minority. This power also enables it to make decisions affecting the incomes, consumption and daily lives of the rest of the community. It is to be remembered that at the present time one of the most powerful weapons in the state's fight against inflation is the threat of severe unemployment. The power of private business over employees can be harnessed by the state to serve its own ends and, therefore, the ends of the business class itself.[11]

It must therefore be of interest to the student of power in Britain that in a modern capitalist economy a small minority controls the main sources of capital and the boards of banks, insurance companies, industrial and service companies and the nationalised industries. Of the top 120 companies the majority are controlled by tycoons or families.[12] Ten of Britain's largest companies are controlled by a single family group. Disparities in income and wealth, 'intimately correlated with personal security, educational opportunity, the scope for travel and recreation, diet, health and the general pleasantness of everyday living',[13] are still very great. The richest 5 per cent of the population own approximately 75 per cent of all private wealth. The top 1 per cent of incomes receives roughly the same share of total income as the bottom *third*. The redistribution of personal incomes towards greater equality stopped in 1957. Since then the trend may have been reversed.[14]

At the bottom end of the social scale it was estimated by a senior Conservative politician in 1970 that between 7 and 10 million people lived on or below the poverty line. 13 million people (nearly a quarter of the population) are dependent on national insurance, supplementary benefits and other social security payments rather than on wages and salaries. The number of unemployed is increasing and they receive lower national insurance benefits than most other beneficiaries. This poverty is a function of class. The low paid, the old, the chronic sick, the disabled, the fatherless families and the unemployed are not poor because they fall into these categories. They are poor because they are working class. 'The basic fact is that the poor are an integral part of the working class — its poorest and most disadvantaged stratum.'[15]

Economic inequality affects not only life style but also political power. Those who lack economic resources tend also to lack other resources relevant to the exercise of political power. Working class people are less likely than middle class people to vote, join political parties, hold political office, or have a high sense of political efficacy, political knowledge or organisational skills or the time to devote to politics.[16] So far as political participation is a function of education it is interesting to note that class differentials in educational opportunity eliminate 96 per cent of manual working class children from formal full-time education before the age of seventeen.

The political deprivation of the poor is often unrecognised. It is assumed that their possession of political rights confers political equality. However such political rights are of little consequence in the face of such impediments to political equality as the lack of political organisation, the weaknesses of pressure groups acting on behalf of the poor, the prevailing values which legitimise inequality, and the administrative culture of the means-tested welfare state which suggests to the poor 'that the war which is being waged is not against poverty but against them'.[17]

A ruling class

A second factor which needs to be taken into account in any analysis of community power structure is the extent to which the state elite has been 'colonised' by the dominant economic class. There is no shortage of evidence that the various elites within the British political system are drawn disproportionately from the upper and middle classes, and that the state, far from acting as an impartial umpire, adjudicating between competing interests, throws its weight behind groups which are already endowed with power by the economic system.

The links between members of the political, administrative, military, judicial, industrial and religious elites encompass social class, educational experience and even kinship. Members of Parliament come from predominantly professional, managerial and propertied backgrounds. As Labour's representation in Parliament has grown the percentage of MPs with a working class background has actually declined and the two major parliamentary parties are becoming similar in terms of class background and career patterns.[18] Cabinet ministers are even more overwhelmingly middle class, under Conservative and Labour administrations alike. The higher one moves through the administrative grades of the civil and diplomatic services, the less likely one is to find senior officials of working class origins. The working class is totally unrepresented among the senior ranks of the Army.[19]

The educational background of elite members further reinforces the bonds of class between the political and other elites. Cabinet ministers, senior civil servants, High Court judges, Anglican bishops, senior Army officers, company directors and leading industrialists tend to be drawn from a very small group of select schools and universities.[20] In this way members of the elite ensure the predominance among them of people from their own class by recruiting from educational establishments which are, for economic and social reasons, closed to the vast majority of children of lower middle and working class parents. Thus while only 2.5 per cent of the population enjoy a public school education, it is this group which fills the majority of positions within the economic elite and the state apparatus. The predominance of Oxford and Cambridge Universities in the educational backgrounds of members of all elites again reflects the narrow social and educational stratum from which they are drawn. When the middle and upper classes purchase public school educations for their children 'they are starting their children on the road to power and influence. The principal commodity which those who send their children to public schools are buying is not education but privilege.'[21]

Kinship is difficult to trace by sociological investigation, but there is some evidence to hand of family connections between members of the state elites. For example, it has been calculated that over 40 per cent of the three top ranks in the British Army are connected by birth or marriage to members of the economic and state elites (major financiers, company directors, peers, Cabinet ministers, senior diplomats and senior civil servants).[22]

How does the socio-economic class which dominates elite positions in both the economy and the state use its power? One way, unrecognised by pluralist approaches to power and decision-making which focus exclusively on policy decisions, is to exclude from the decision-making arena major issues which would threaten its interests. There is so little empirical evidence to turn to here that it is only possible to pose a series of questions which must be asked when attempting to complete the analysis of power in a political system by going beyond the determination of policies or the making of decisions. How can an interest exercise power by devoting its energies 'to creating or reinforcing social and political values and institutional practices that limit the scope of the political process to public consideration of only those issues which are comparatively innocuous'?[23] Does the ruling class manipulate the rest of the society by 'tactical concessions' or by 'domination of the mental environment'? Are there dominant social values which consistently favour capitalism and Conservatism rather than socialism and Labour? Do the economically privileged legitimate inequalities in the minds of the underprivileged by 'engineering consent'?

The proposition, however, that the dominant economic interests use their 'colonisation' of the state to protect themselves is supported by some evidence. The boards of banks, insurance companies and industrial enterprises provide places for ex-Cabinet ministers and senior civil servants. Large numbers of industrialists are in their turn brought into government to serve on advisory bodies, the boards of nationalised industries and other public agencies, and as ministerial advisers. This has been offered as an explanation of why public enterprises have been prevented from expansion when this was contrary to the interests of private capital, and why in general the nationalised industries have been 'subordinated to the needs of a predominantly capitalist economy'.[24] It is a distinctive feature of all capitalist systems that businessmen participate in the management of public concerns and the formulation of public policies for the private sector.

Incrementalism or planning?

Finally, the association between pluralism and incrementalism must be looked upon with a critical eye. This is because the theory of decision-making known as incrementalism can easily turn into a political theory known as conservatism. The proposition that because of behavioural constraints policy-making *can* only proceed by consider-ing a limited range of small changes is easily converted to an imperative that policies *should* be made in this way. When marginal change is satisfactory to those in power and there is a high degree of continuity in their perceptions of the problems and the means of dealing with them, then incrementalism may suffice. When, on the other hand, radical change is sought, the past by definition offers no basis on which to build. New means to the solution of new problems have to be found. Similarly when consensus is absent from the political system incremental change may be politically impossible. There are obvious ideological overtones to a theory of policy-making which sees agreement on a policy as a criterion of its quality, for it clearly assumes consensus rather than conflict as the distinguishing feature of the policy-making process, or that the only conflict is over means and not ends. Incrementalism is 'an ideological reinforcement of the pro-inertia and anti-innovation forces prevalent in all human organisations, administrative and policy making'.[25] Whether it is possible to achieve as much change and as rapidly through a sequence of incremental steps as through more radical innovation depends entirely on the type of change being defined. That in itself is an ideological issue.

CONCLUSION

This discussion has strayed far from the process of policy-making into the notoriously difficult area of power in the modern state. It has skirted round the theoretical problems associated with all elitist theories of power, and the controversies, both scientific and ideological, which abound over the relationship between economic resources and economic power, and between economic and political power.[26] Such issues deserve much more systematic treatment than can be given here or, it may be said, than they are usually given elsewhere. However it is hoped that this chapter will make students of public policy-making more aware than they might have been of the structure of power within which issues and problems arise or are prevented from arising, and within which the determination of final decisions is achieved for those issues which do enter the political arena.

There is a very real gap in the literature on political power in Britain which is revealed when this point is considered. On the one hand the exercise of power in specific decision-making processes has received some attention. On the other the factors which give large social groupings a potential for power, such as economic strength or domination of the state apparatus, have been examined. But assessments of the significance of class and wealth in the determination of particular issues have not been made. Outcomes favourable to specified groups have been assumed to be the consequences of the power of those groups. For example, the absence of socialist reform in Britain and the continued dominance of the propertied class is ascribed to the power of that class. In view of the changes which have taken place in the political and constitutional systems, such as the rise of trade unionism, extensions of the franchise, mass literacy and the share of office enjoyed by the Labour Party since the Second World War, which theoretically place political power in the hands of the working class, the continued dominance of the middle and upper-middle classes can only be explained by reference to engineered legitimacy by which representatives of the propertied classes have been able to maintain a disproportionate control of the offices of state. What remains for empirical investigation is to test how pressure and influence are exerted on specific policy issues by economic interests through their occupancy of elite positions within the state apparatus. How does ownership of the means of production affect ownership of the means of decision-making? This question reveals that the study of power and therefore the study of public policy-making ultimately demands an assessment of all aspects of the political system.[27] Studies of political institutions, the machinery of government and decision-making processes must be carried out within a framework of power as it is exercised in all social relationships.

References

CHAPTER 1

1 See, for example, D. Easton 'An Approach to the Analysis of Political Systems' *World Politics*, IX: 1 (1957) and *The Political System*, New York Alfred A. Knopf (1953)
2 For an excellent example of the use to which systems analysis can be put in the study of British politics see H. V. Wiseman *Politics in Everyday Life* Oxford, Basil Blackwell (1966)
3 Charles E. Lindblom *The Policy-Making Process* New York, Prentice-Hall (1968) p. 4
4 *Ibid.* pp. 30–1

CHAPTER 2

1 Sir Charles Cunningham 'Policy and Practice' *Public Administration* XLI: (1963) 229–38
2 Y. Dror *Public Policy Making Re-examined* San Francisco, Chandler (1968)
3 Morton Kroll 'Policy and Administration' in F. J. Lyden, G. A. Shipman and M. Kroll *Policies, Decisions and Organisation* New York, Appleton-Century-Crofts, (1969)
4 Sir Geoffrey Vickers *The Art of Judgement* London, Chapman & Hall, (1965)
5 W. C. Mitchell 'The Structural Characteristics of policy making', in Lyden, Shipman and Kroll *op. cit.*
6 Dror *op. cit.* p. 14
7 Peter Self *Administrative Theories and Politics* London, Allen & Unwin (1972) p. 67
8 Lindblom *op. cit.* p. 4
9 P. Bachrach and M. Baratz 'Two faces of power' *American Political Science Review,* LVI (1962) pp. 947–52
10 Evelyn Sharp *The Ministry of Housing and Local Government,* London, Allen & Unwin (1969) pp. 75–7
11 D. Keeling *Management in Government* London, Allen & Unwin (1972) p. 24
12 Dror *op. cit.* p. 14
13 Self *op. cit.* p. 149
14 *Ibid.* p. 26
15 A. Ranney 'The Study of Policy Content: A Framework for Choice', in Ranney (ed.) *Political Science and Public Policy*, Chicago, Markham (1968)

16 R. H. Tawney *Equality*, London, Allen & Unwin (1931) p. 229; see also A. de Crespigny 'Power and its forms' *Political Studies*, XVI (1968)
17 D. M. White 'The Problem of Power' *British Journal of Political Science* II: 4 (1972) p. 482
18 Robert Michels *Political Parties* New York, Collier Books (1962) p. 70
19 C. W. Cassinelli 'Political Authority: its exercise and possession' *Western Political Quarterly* XIV: 3 (1961) pp. 636—7
20 John Day 'Authority' *Political Studies* XI: 3 (1963) p. 258
21 Max Weber *The Theory of Social and Economic Organisation* ed. Talcott Parsons Glencoe, Ill.: The Free Press (1947) p. 364
22 Max Weber 'The Three Types of Legitimate Rule' reprinted in A. Etzioni, *A Sociological Reader on Complex Organisations* New York, Holt, Rinehart & Winston (1969) p. 9
23 *Ibid*.
24 Day *op. cit.* p. 258
25 c.f. P. H. Partridge 'Some notes on the concept of power' *Political Studies* XI (1963)
26 Graham Wootton *Interest-Groups* New York, Prentice-Hall (1970) pp. 75—6
27 See W. A. Gamson *Power and Discontent* London, Dorsey Press (1968) pp. 59—85, reprinted in F. G. Castles, D. J. Murray and D. C. Potter (eds) *Decisions, Organisations and Society* Harmondsworth, Penguin (1971)
28 de Crespigny *op. cit.*
29 Wootton *op. cit.* pp. 78—9
30 Herbert A. Simon *Administrative Behaviour* 2nd edn, New York, The Free Press (1957) p. xxiv
31 Herbert A. Simon, Donald W. Smithburg and Victor A. Thompson *Public Administration* New York, Knopf (1958) p. 423
32 Simon, *op. cit.* p. 4
33 *Ibid.* p. 5
34 *Ibid.* p. 14
35 *Ibid.* p. 39

CHAPTER 3

1 Lindblom *op. cit.* ch. 5
2 Peter Bromhead *Britain's Developing Constitution* London, Allen & Unwin (1974) p. 7
3 R. Rose *Politics in England* London, Faber (1965) ch. 2
4 D. Pickles *Democracy* London, Methuen (1971) p. 13
5 A. H. Birch *Representative and Responsible Government* London, Allen & Unwin (1964) p. 17
6 *Ibid.* p. 15
7 S. I. Benn and R. S. Peters *Social Principles and the Democratic State* London, Allen & Unwin (1959) p. 344
8 D. Pickles *op. cit.* p. 156
9 A. H. Birch *op. cit.* p. 19
10 *Ibid.* p. 21
11 *Ibid.* pp. 241—2
12 J. S. Mill *Representative Government* Everyman edn, London, Dent (1910) pp. 347—8

13 A. H. Birch *The British System of Government* London, Allen & Unwin (1967) ch. 2
14 R. M. Punnett *British Government and Politics* London, Heinemann (1968) p. 22
15 S. E. Finer *Comparative Government* Harmondsworth, Penguin (1970) p. 131
16 S. E. Finer *The Man on Horseback* London, Pall Mall Press (1962) p. 87
17 G. Almond and S. Verba *The Civic Culture* Princeton, NJ, Princeton UP (1963) p. 490
18 *Ibid.*
19 Benn and Peters *op. cit.* p. 353
20 Mill *op. cit.* p. 209
21 *Ibid.* p. 208
22 Dror *op. cit.* p. 165
23 J. K. Friend and W. N. Jessop *Local Government and Strategic Choice* London, Tavistock (1969) p. 105
24 M. Meyerson and E. Banfield *Politics, Planning and the Public Interest* Glencoe Ill., The Free Press (1955) p. 316
25 Dror *op. cit.* p. 138
26 Friend and Jessop *op cit.* p. 116
27 W. G. Scott, *Organisation Theory* Homewood, Ill. Irwin (1967) reprinted in Castles, Murray and Potter *op. cit.* p. 21
28 *Ibid.* p. 24
29 Friend and Jessop *op. cit.* pp. 88—97 and 106—8
30 *Ibid.* p. 89
31 *Ibid.* p. 116
32 *Ibid.* p. 111
33 *Ibid.* p. 110

CHAPTER 4

1 Almond and Verba *op. cit.* p. 219
2 David Butler and Donald Stokes *Political Change in Britain* Harmondsworth, Penguin (1971) p. 42; Almond and Verba *op. cit.* p. 129
3 Mill *op. cit.* p. 228
4 Peter G. J. Pulzer *Political Representation and Elections in Britain* London, Allen & Unwin (1972) p. 96
5 Butler and Stokes *op. cit.* p. 49
6 *Ibid.* p. 228
7 *Ibid.* p. 411
8 *Ibid.* pp. 411—12
9 *Ibid.* p. 412
10 Birch *op. cit.* pp. 190—1
11 See Pulzer *op. cit.* pp. 135—8 for a discussion of rationality and voting
12 Butler and Stokes *op. cit* p. 42; see also G. C. Moodie and G. Studdert-Kennedy *Opinions, Publics and Pressure Groups* London, Allen & Unwin (1970) p. 21. However, for qualification see R. J. Benewick *et al.* 'The floating voter and the liberal view of representation' *Political Studies* XVII: 2 (1969)
13 Pulzer *op. cit.* pp. 122—3

14 Butler and Stokes *op. cit.* p. 242
15 *Ibid.* pp. 248—64
16 *Ibid.* ch. 12
17 A. H. Hanson and M. Walles *Governing Britain* London, Fontana (1970) ch. 2; Pulzer *op. cit.* pp. 50—60; Wiseman *op. cit.* pp. 83—5
18 Speech to the Conference on Industrial Relations in the Health Service, 21 October 1974, quoted in *Red Tape* (December 1974) p. 71
19 S. A. Walkland *The Legislative Process in Great Britain* London, Allen & Unwin (1968) pp. 22—3
20 R. Rose and H. Mossawir 'Voting and Elections: a functional analysis' *Political Studies* XV: 2 (1967) p. 198
21 A. Peacock and J. Wiseman *The Growth of Public Expenditure in the United Kingdom* London, Oxford University Press (1961)
22 R. Rose 'The Variability of Party Government' *Political Studies* XVII: 4 (1969) p. 427
23 Peter Fletcher 'The Results Analysed', in L. J. Sharpe *Voting in Cities* London, Macmillan (1967) p. 321
24 R. Gregory 'Local elections and the 'Rule of Anticipated Reactions' ' *Political Studies* XVII: 1 (1969)
25 Butler and Stokes *op. cit.* p. 58
26 R. Rose *Politics in England* London, Faber (1965) ch. 2
27 Almond and Verba *op. cit.* pp. 141—2
28 Butler and Stokes *op. cit.* p. 50
29 Almond and Verba *op. cit.* p. 160
30 Rose and Mossawir *op. cit.*
31 Rose *Politics in England op. cit.* ch. 2
32 A. King 'Ideas, Institutions and the Policies of Governments. Part III' *British Journal of Political Science* III: 4 (1973)
33 Lord Windlesham 'Can public opinion influence government', in R. Rose (ed.) *Studies in British Politics* London, Macmillan (1969) p. 188
34 Colin Seymour-Ure *The Political Impact of the Mass Media* London, Constable (1974) ch. 8
35 Ralph Miliband *The State in Capitalist Society* London, Weidenfeld & Nicolson (1969) pp. 221—5
36 Seymour-Ure *op. cit.* pp. 166—7
37 *Ibid.* p. 168
38 Colin Seymour-Ure *The Press, Politics and the Public* London, Methuen (1968)
39 Seymour-Ure *The Political Impact of the Mass Media* p. 203; see also Butler and Stokes *op. cit.* pp. 286—7
40 J. Trenaman and D. McQuail *Television and the Political Image* London, Methuen (1961) p. 234
41 J. G. Blumler and D. McQuail *Television in Politics: Its uses and influences* London, Faber (1968) ch. 4
42 *Ibid.* pp. 216—17
43 D. E. Butler 'Political Reporting in Britain' in R. Rose (ed). *Studies in British Politics* London, Macmillan (1969)
44 See D. M. Hill *Democratic Theory and Local Government* London, Allen & Unwin, (1974) pp. 173—9
45 R. T. McKenzie 'Parties, Pressure Groups and The British Political Process' *Political Quarterly* (1958)
46 G. K. Roberts *Political Parties and Pressure Groups in Britain* London, Weidenfeld & Nicolson (1970) pp. 91—6

47 W. Plowden *The Motor Car and Politics 1896—1970* London, Bodley Head (1971) p. 376

48 *Ibid.* p. 372

49 Address by Mr M. Carlisle to the Annual General Meeting of the Howard League, 24 November 1970

50 Plowden *op. cit.* p. 375

51 J. Dearlove *The Politics of Policy in Local Government* Cambridge, CUP (1973) ch. 8

52 *Cf.* Bridget Pym *Pressure Groups and the Permissive Society* Newton Abbot, David & Charles (1974)

53 Plowden *op. cit.* pp. 372—3 and 376—7

54 A. Silkin 'Green Papers and Changing Methods of Consultation in British Government' *Public Administration* (winter 1973)

55 See, for an example, W. P. Grant and D. Marsh 'The Confederation of British Industry' *Political Studies* XIX: 4 (1971)

56 The *ad hoc* species is now thoroughly covered by R. A. Chapman *The Role of Commissions in Policy Making* London, Allen & Unwin (1973) and G. Rhodes *Committees of Inquiry,* London, Allen & Unwin (1975); see also K. C. Wheare *Government by Committee* Oxford, Clarendon Press (1955); T. J. Cartwright *Royal Commissions and Departmental Committees in Britain* London, University of London Press (1974); and PEP *Advisory Committees in British Government* London, Allen & Unwin (1960)

57 Grant and Marsh *op. cit.* p. 409

58 R. Klein 'Policy-making in the national health service' *Political Studies* XXII: 1 (1974) p. 6

CHAPTER 5

1 R. Rose 'The Political Ideas of English Party Activists' in Rose (ed.) *Studies in British Politics* p. 390

2 R. McKenzie *British Political Parties* London, Heinemann (1963) pp. 62—8; M. Pinto-Duschinsky 'Central Office and "Power" in the Conservative Party' *Political Studies* XX: 1 (1972)

3 Mackenzie *ibid.* p. 635

4 R. M. Punnett *Front-Bench Opposition* London, Heinemann (1973) pp. 129—31

5 Dick Leonard 'How Candidates are Chosen' in D. Leonard and V. Herman *The Backbencher and Parliament* London, Macmillan (1972) p. 20

6 D. M. Hill *op. cit.* p. 70

7 See, for example, F. Bealey, J. Blondel and W. P. McCann *Constituency Politics* London, Faber (1965) pp. 370—9

8 Sir Ivor Jennings *Parliament* Cambridge, Cambridge UP (1969) p. 8

9 E. C. S. Wade and G. G. Phillips *Constitutional Law* London, Longman (1960) p. 49

10 *Study of Parliament Group Memorandum to the Select Committee on Procedure, Fourth Report,* 1964—5 session H. C. 393, p. 139

11 P. G. Richards *The Reformed Local Government System* London, Allen & Unwin (1973) pp. 148—57

12 See R. E. Dowse and T. Smith 'Party Discipline in the House of Commons —

A Comment' *Parliamentary Affairs* (1963); Richard Rose *Politics in England* London, Faber (1965) p. 199

13 P. A. Bromhead *Private Members' Bills in the British Parliament* London, Routledge (1956) p. 171
14 David McKie 'Is this democracy?' *Guardian* (5 May 1972)
15 Jennings *op. cit.* pp. 478–9; S. A. Walkland *The Legislative Process in Great Britain* London, Allen & Unwin (1968) p. 44
16 Walkland *op. cit.* London, pp. 89–90
17 R. Butt *The Power of Parliament* London, Constable (1969) pp. 188 and 196
18 *Ibid.* pp. 214–15
19 *Ibid.* pp. 232–3
20 See J. P. Mackintosh's analysis of Labour MPs' rebellions in the 1967–9 sessions in 'Parliament now and a Hundred Years Ago' in Leonard and Herman *op. cit.*
21 Butt *op. cit.* pp. 317–18
22 Punnett *op. cit.* pp. 183 and 198
23 Butt *op. cit.* p. 319
24 *Ibid.* pp. 323–4
25 *Ibid.* p. 318; see also Punnett *op. cit.* especially ch. 1
26 Punnett *ibid.* p. 204. On the use of the Lords' few remaining powers in recent years see P. Bromhead *Britain's Developing Constitutions* London, Allen & Unwin (1974) ch. 18
27 P. G. Richards *The Backbenchers* London, Faber (1972) p. 149
28 See N. Johnson *Parliament and Administration* London, Allen & Unwin (1966); A. Morris (ed.) *The Growth of Parliamentary Scrutiny by Committee* Oxford, Pergamon (1970); A. Hanson and B. Crick (eds) *The Commons in Transition* London, Collins (1970); Butt *op. cit.* ch. 13; D. Coombes *The Member of Parliament and the Administration* London, Allen & Unwin (1966)
29 Butt *op. cit.* p. 382
30 *Ibid.* p. 308
31 *Ibid.*; see also Peter Jenkins *The Battle of Downing Street* London, Charles Knight (1970)

CHAPTER 6

1 Lindblom *op. cit.* p. 30
2 J. P. Mackintosh *The British Cabinet* London, Methuen, 2nd ed (1968) p. 3
3 Sir Ivor Jennings *Cabinet Government* Cambridge, Cambridge UP 3rd ed (1969) p. 1
4 Mackintosh *op. cit.* p. 16; see also p. 521. For recent developments see Bromhead *op. cit.*, pp. 74–8
5 Jennings *op. cit.* p. 245
6 G. W. Jones 'The Prime Minister's Power' *Parliamentary Affairs* XVIII (spring 1965); R. W. K. Hinton 'The Prime Minister as an Elected Monarch' *Parliamentary Affairs* XIII (summer 1960); D. N. Chester 'Who Governs Britain?' *Parliamentary Affairs* XV: 4 (1962); R. H. S. Crossman, introduction to Walter Bagehot's *The English Constitution* London, Fontana (1963); A. H. Brown 'Prime Ministerial Power', parts I and II, *Public Law* (spring and summer 1968); Mackintosh, *op. cit.*

194   *Policy-Making in British Government*

7 Brown *op. cit.*
8 For an example of this view see Patrick Gordon Walker *The Cabinet* London, Fontana (1972) p. 79
9 Jones *op. cit.* pp. 177—8
10 Brown *op. cit.* Part II, pp. 106—7
11 *Ibid.* p. 113
12 Crossman *op. cit.* p. 52
13 *Ibid.* p. 184
14 Gordon Walker *op. cit.* pp. 96—7
15 Brown *op. cit.* p. 99
16 Mackintosh *op. cit.* p. 623
17 *Ibid.* pp. 434—5
18 Brown *op. cit.* p. 36
19 *Ibid.* Part II, p. 100
20 Brown *op. cit.* Part I, p. 44
21 H. Heclo and A. Wildavsky *The Private Government of Public Money* London, Macmillan (1974) p. 317
22 *Ibid.* p. 323
23 Richard Crossman *The Diaries of a Cabinet Minister* vol. 1, Minister of Housing 1964—66, London, Cape, (1975), p. 249
24 Heclo and Wildavsky *op. cit.* p. 368
25 Mackintosh *op. cit.* pp. 3—11
26 B. Heady *British Cabinet Ministers* London, Allen & Unwin (1974) pp. 158—9
27 See, for example, Edward Boyle and Anthony Crosland in conversation with Maurice Kogan *The Politics of Education* Harmondsworth, Penguin (1971) p. 41
28 The Fulton Committee *The Civil Service* II, London, HMSO (1968) p. 13
29 Walkland *op. cit.* p. 23
30 Rose 'The variability of party government' pp. 425—6
31 J. Bray *Decision in Government* London, Gollancz (1969) p. 52
32 Bagehot *op. cit.* p. 201
33 Heady *op. cit.* p. 63
34 *The Politics of Education op. cit.* p. 43
35 Peter Shore *Entitled to Know* quoted in Rose 'The Variability of Party Government' p. 428
36 Heady *op. cit.* p. 176; see also Crossman *The Diaries of a Cabinet Minister op. cit.*
37 *Ibid.* pp. 181—2
38 S. Brittan *Steering the Economy* Harmondsworth, Penguin (1971) pp. 55—6; Heady *op. cit.* pp. 182—7
39 Heady *op. cit.* p. 187
40 Heady *op. cit.* p. 174
41 Crossman *The Diaries of a Cabinet Minister op. cit.*
42 *Ibid.* p. 90
43 *The Politics of Education* p. 43; Heady *op. cit.* p. 173
44 *The Politics of Education op. cit.* p. 48; see also D. N. Chester 'The Wartime Machine', in R. Rose (ed.) *Policy-Making in Britain* London, Macmillan (1969)
45 Sir Richard Clarke *New Trends in Government* London HMSO (1971)
46 Crossman *op. cit.*
47 Rose 'The Variability of Party Government' *op. cit.* p. 423; Heady *op. cit.* pp. 40—1
48 Rose *ibid.* p. 420

49 Heady *op. cit.* pp. 36—8
50 Report of a Study Group on Local Authority Management Structures (*Bains Report*) *The New Local Authorities* London, HMSO (1972) para. 3.8
51 *Ibid.* ch. 3
52 Bray *op. cit.* pp. 62—3
53 The Fulton Committee *The Civil Service* I, Cmnd. 3638 London, HMSO (1968)
54 Brittan *op. cit.* p. 53
55 Heady *op. cit.* p. 215
56 Rose 'The Variability of Party Government' pp. 441—3
57 F. L. Morrison *Courts and the Political Process in England* London, Sage Publications (1973) pp. 86—7
58 *Ibid.* p. 97
59 For cases, see J. A. G. Griffith 'Judges in Politics: England' *Government and Opposition* III: 4 (1968)
60 H. J. Elcock 'Justice and the Political Order' *Political Studies* XVII: 3 (1969)
61 Morrison *op. cit.* pp. 162—6
62 Sir Leslie Scarman 'Law and Administration: A Change in Relationship' *Public Administration* L (autumn 1972) p. 254
63 *Ibid.* p. 258
64 B. Abel-Smith and R. Stevens *Lawyers and the Courts* London, Heinemann (1967) pp. 299—310

CHAPTER 7

1 J. A. G. Griffith *Central Departments and Local Authorities* London, Allen & Unwin (1966) pp. 511—14
2 For a summary of these assumptions, see N. T. Boaden *Urban Policy-Making* Cambridge, Cambridge UP (1971) pp. 11—13
3 D. E. Ashford 'The effects of central finance on the British local government system' *British Journal of Political Science* IV: No. 197, p. 320
4 E. James 'Frontiers in the Welfare State' *Public Administration* XLIV (winter 1966); B. Davies 'Local Authority size: some associations with standards of performance of services for deprived children and old people' *Public Administration* XLVII (summer 1969); B. Davies 'Welfare Departments and Territorial Justice: some implications for the reform of local government' *Social and Economic Administration* III: 4 (1969)
5 Boaden *op. cit.* ch. 2
6 Boaden *op. cit.*
7 Boaden *op. cit.* chs 5—9; see also Noel Boaden and R. T. Alford 'Sources of Diversity in English Local Government Decisions' *Public Administration* XLVII (summer 1969)
8 F. R. Oliver and J. Stanyer 'Some aspects of the financial behaviour of county boroughs' *Public Administration* XLVII (summer 1969)
9 Boaden *op. cit.* pp. 102—3
10 Oliver and Stanyer *op. cit.*
11 N. T. Boaden 'Innovation and Change in English Local Government' *Political Studies* XIX: 4 (1971) p. 428
12 Boaden *Urban Policy-Making* p. 70
13 *Ibid.* p. 96

14 J. E. Alt 'Some social and political correlates of county borough expenditures' *British Journal of Political Science* I: 1 (1971) p. 60
15 Boaden *Urban Policy-Making* p. 106
16 *Ibid.* p. 93
17 Boaden 'Innovation and Change in English Local Government p. 424
18 B. Davies *Social Needs and Resources in Local Services* London, Michael Joseph (1968)
19 B. Davies 'Local Authority Size: some associations with standards of performance of services for deprived children and old people' *Public Administration* XLVII (summer 1969)
20 *Ibid.* p. 243
21 See Andrew Gray 'The study of public policy in local government: some reflections for British political science' *Public Administration Bulletin* XVII (June 1975)
22 Boaden *Urban Policy-Making* p. 20

CHAPTER 8

1 *Bains Report* p. 83
2 T. Eddison *Local Government: Management and Corporate Planning* Aylesbury, Leonard Hill Books (1973) p. 9
3 Sir William Pile 'Corporate Planning for Education in the Department of Education and Science' *Public Administration* LII (spring 1974) p. 13
4 C. E. Mills 'Corporate Planning in the British Gas Corporation' *Public Administration* LII (spring 1974) p. 28
5 J. Garrett *The Management of Government* Harmondsworth, Penguin (1972) p. 115; see also A. W. Peterson 'Planning, Programming and Budgeting in the GLC: What and Why' *Public Administration*, L (summer 1972)
6 G. J. Wasserman 'Planning Programming Budgeting in the Police Service in England and Wales' *O and M Bulletin* XXV: 4 (1970) p. 204
7 Sir Samuel Goldman *Public Expenditure Management and Control* (Civil Service College Studies no. 2) London, HMSO (1973) p. 46
8 *Ibid.* pp. 50–1
9 See, for example, Department of Education and Science *Output Budgeting for the Department of Education and Science* London, HMSO (1970) p. 3
10 Alan Williams *Output Budgeting and the contribution of micro-economics to efficiency in government* (CAS Occasional Paper no. 4) London, HMSO (1967) p. 14; see also p. 7, para. 13
11 Garrett *op. cit.* p. 121
12 Department of Education and Science *op. cit.* p. 109
13 Eddison *op. cit.* pp. 59 and 76–9
14 Williams *op. cit.* pp. 10–11
15 For further details see Garrett *op. cit.* pp. 104–7; *Public Expenditure: Planning and Control* Cmnd. 2915 London, HMSO (1966); and Select Committee on Procedure *The Planning and Control of Public Expenditure* session 1968–9, H.C. 410
16 J. M. Bridgeman 'Planning–Programming–Budgeting Systems, Part I' *O and M Bulletin* XXIV: 4 (1969) pp. 172–3
17 See Ann Robinson 'Prospects for PPBS: Some macro-political variables examined for USA, Canada and Britain' *PAC Bulletin*, XII (June 1972)

18 Sir Samuel Goldman 'New Techniques in Government Budgeting: 1. The Presentation of Public Expenditure Proposals to Parliament' *Public Administration* XLVIII (autumn 1970) p. 255

19 Garrett *op. cit.* pp. 136—7

20 Goldman *Public Expenditure Management and Control op. cit.* p. 49; see also E. A. Collins 'The functional approach to public expenditure' *Public Administration* XLIV (autumn 1966)

21 Select Committee on Procedure *op. cit.* p. 261

22 R. Klein 'The Politics of PPB' *Political Quarterly* XLIII: 3 (1972)

23 Eddison *op. cit.* p. 63

24 Department of Education and Science *op. cit.* pp. 17—18

25 J. M. Bridgeman 'Planning-Programming-Budgeting Systems, Part II' *O and M Bulletin* XXV: 1 (1970)

26 Bridgeman *op. cit.* 'Part I', p. 170

27 Bridgeman *op. cit.* 'Part II'

28 Department of Education and Science *op. cit.* p. 10

29 Eddison *op. cit.* p. 168

30 Garrett *op. cit.* pp. 130 and 137—8

31 Select Committee on Procedure *op. cit.*, memorandum by the Treasury on 'Output Budgeting' p. 188

32 Wasserman *op. cit.*

33 See Eddison *op. cit.* ch. 7; R. Greenwood, J. D. Stewart and A. D. Smith 'The Policy Committee in English Local Government' *Public Administration* L (summer 1972); and 'Corporate Planning and the Chief Officers' Group' *Local Government Studies* (October 1971); and the *Bains Report*

34 Goldman *Public Expenditure Management & Control* p. 36; see also Heclo and Wildavsky *op. cit.* pp. 217—18

35 Heclo and Wildavsky *op. cit.* p. 227

36 *Ibid.* p. 296

37 Klein 'The Politics of PPB' *op. cit.* p. 274

38 A Financial Secretary to the Treasury quoted in Heclo and Wildavsky *op. cit.* p. 24

39 J. G. Bagley 'Planning, Programming Budgeting in DES' *O and M Bulletin* XXVII: 2 (1972)

CHAPTER 9

1 *Nationalised Industries: A Review of Economic and Financial Objectives* Cmnd. 3437 London, HMSO (1967)

2 *Public Expenditure: Planning and Control* Cmnd. 2915 London, HMSO (1966)

3 C. D. Foster *The Transport Problem* London, Blackie (1963) quoted in G. H. Peters *Cost-Benefit Analysis and Public Expenditure* London, Institute of Economic Affairs (1973) p. 29

4 H. M. Treasury *Forestry in Great Britain, An Interdepartmental Cost-Benefit Study* London, HMSO (1972)

5 D. W. Pearce *Cost-Benefit Analysis* London, Macmillan (1971) p. 9. See also M. S. Feldstein 'Cost-Benefit Analysis and Investment in the Public Sector' *Public Administration* XLII (winter 1964) pp. 352—3

6 For a layman's introduction to CBA see T. Newton *Cost-Benefit Analysis in Administration* London, Allen & Unwin (1972)

7 Feldstein *op. cit.*

8 Friend and Jessop *op. cit.* pp. 92—3

9 *Ibid.* pp. 139—40; E. K. G. James 'Operational Research in Government' *O and M Bulletin* XXV: 2 (1970) p. 85

10 Friend and Jessop *op. cit.* pp. 193—5 and 237—8

11 Feldstein *op. cit* p. 356

12 Pearce *op. cit.* p. 55. On the problem of valuation for the Roskill Commission on the third London airport, see the critique by Peter Self ' "Nonsense on Stilts": Cost-Benefit Analysis and the Roskill Commission' *Political Quarterly* XLI: (July 1970). For a reaction to this criticism from an economist, see Alan Williams 'Cost-Benefit Analysis: Bastard Science and/or insidious poison in the body politick?' *Journal of Public Economics* I: 2 (1972)

13 Pearce *op. cit.* pp. 52—4

14 *Ibid.* pp. 26—31

15 A. Wildavsky 'The Political Economy of Efficiency: Cost-Benefit Analysis, Systems Analysis and Program Budgeting' *Public Administration Review* XXVI: 4 (December 1966) p. 294

16 This case study is drawn from Ministry of Transport *Report of a study of Rail Links with Heathrow Airport* part II, London, HMSO (1970)

17 *Ibid.* p. 63

18 A. R. Prest and R. Turvey 'Cost-Benefit Analysis: A Survey' *Economic Journal* LXXV (December 1965)

CHAPTER 10

1 M. Olson 'The plan and purpose of a Social Report' *The Public Interest* XV (spring 1969) p. 92

2 Eighth Report from the Expenditure Committee, Session 1971—72, *Relationship of Expenditure to Needs* HC 515 (1972) p. vi

3 *Ibid.* pp. 78—9

4 *Ibid.* p. xi

5 'A textbook city fails the test' *Guardian* (17 April 1975)

6 Mark Abrams 'Subjective Social Indicators' *Social Trends* IV London, HMSO (1973)

7 Eighth Report from the Expenditure Committee, *op. cit.* p. ix

8 Olson *op. cit.* p. 88

9 *Ibid.* p. 90

10 A. J. Culyer, R. J. Lavers and A. Williams 'Social Indicators: Health' *Social Trends* II London, HMSO (1971) p. 39. See also Klein 'The Politics of PPB'

11 C. A. Moser 'Some general developments in social statistics' *Social Trends* I London, HMSO (1970) p. 7

12 *Ibid.* p. 10

13 Ministry of Reconstruction *Report of the Machinery of Government Committee* Cd. 9230 (1918); *The Civil Service* I, Cmnd. 3638 (1968)

14 *The Reorganization of Central Government* (White Paper) Cmnd. 4506 (1970)

15 C. Pollitt 'The Central Policy Review Staff 1970—74' *Public Administration* LII (winter 1974) pp. 378—9. See also W. Plowden 'The Central Policy Review Staff: The first two years', paper delivered to Political Studies Association Conference (March 1973); and 'The role and limits of a central planning staff in government: a note on the Central Policy Review Staff', paper delivered to the Birmingham University Conference on the Study of Public Policy (1973)

16 G. K. Fry 'Policy-Planning Units in British Central Government Departments' *Public Administration* L (summer 1972)
17 Eddison *op. cit.* pp. 162–3
18 Third Report from the Expenditure Committee, Session 1970–71, *Command Papers on Public Expenditure* HC 549 (1971) p. 146
19 Eighth Report from the Expenditure Committee, p. x
20 M. Flynn, P. Flynn and N. Mellor 'Social malaise research: a study in Liverpool' *Social Trends* III London, HMSO (1972)
21 'Statistics revolt by resentful councils' *Guardian* (15 May 1975)
22 Charles E. Lindblom *The Intelligence of Democracy* New York, Collier-Macmillan (1965) p. 139. On the 'costs' of information generally, see R. Rose 'The market for policy indicators' in A. Schonfield and S. Shaw (eds) *Social Indicators & Social Policy* London, Heinemann (1972)
23 Simon *op. cit.* pp. 81–3
24 A. Downs *Inside Bureaucracy* Boston, Little, Brown (1967) pp. 180–3
25 Heclo and Wildavsky *op. cit.* pp. 292–3
26 A. Cherns 'Social sciences and policy', in A. Cherns R. Sinclair and W. I. Jenkins (eds) *Social Sciences and Government* London, Tavistock (1972) p. 19
27 *Ibid.* p. 23
28 R. Klein 'Policy problems and policy perceptions in the National Health Service', paper delivered to the Birmingham University Conference on the Study of Public Policy (1973) pp. 6–7
29 Anthony Forder *Concepts in Social Administration* London, Routledge & Kegan Paul (1974) pp. 53–4
30 Klein *op. cit.* p. 15
31 Olson *op. cit.* p. 92
32 Abrams *op. cit.*
33 Eighth Report from the Expenditure Committee, p. 70
34 'Scandal of death on duty' *Sunday Times* (9 February 1975)
35 F. M. M. Lewes 'Social Trends and Sociological Method' *Social and Economic Administration* V: 3 (1971) p. 177
36 Moser *op. cit.* pp. 10–11
37 Eighth Report from the Expenditure Committee, pp. 70–1
38 P. M. Blau and W. R. Scott *Formal Organisations* London, Routledge & Kegan Paul (1963) pp. 116–19
39 *Ibid.* pp. 121–8

CHAPTER 11

1 Miliband *op. cit.* p. 2
2 C. Hewitt 'Policy-making in Postwar Britain: a Nation-Level test of Elitist and Pluralist Hypotheses' *British Journal of Political Science* IV: 2 (1974)
3 C. A. R. Crosland *The Future of Socialism* London, Cape (1964) ch. 1
4 T. B. Bottomore *Elites and Society* Harmondsworth, Penguin (1966) ch. 6
5 S. H. Beer *Modern British Politics* London, Faber (1965) p. 388
6 Peter Self 'Is comprehensive planning possible and rational?', paper delivered to the Conference on the Study of Public Policy, University of Birmingham (September 1973) p. 3
7 Charles E. Lindblom 'The Science of "Muddling Through" ' *Public Administration Review* XIX: 2 (1959), reprinted in A. Etzioni *Readings on modern organizations* Englewood Cliffs, N.J., Prentice-Hall (1969) p. 160

8　Trevor Smith *Anti-Politics: Consensus, Reform and Protest in Britain* London, Charles Knight (1972)

9　*Ibid.* p. 172

10　S. E. Finer, 'The political power of private capital' in Castles, Murray and Potter *op. cit.* p. 344

11　*Ibid.* pp. 344—5

12　Michael Barratt Brown 'The Controllers of British Industry' in J. Urry and J. Wakeford *Power in Britain* London, Heinemann (1973) pp. 73—103

13　Robin Blackburn 'The Unequal Society' in Urry and Wakeford, *op. cit.* p. 17

14　Urry and Wakeford *op. cit.* chs. 1, 2 and 4

15　R. Miliband 'Politics and Poverty' in D. Wedderburn (ed.) *Poverty, Inequality and Class Structure* Cambridge, CUP (1974) p. 185

16　R. E. Dowse and S. A. Hughes *Political Sociology* London, Wiley (1972) p. 140

17　*Ibid.* p. 189

18　W. L. Guttsman 'The British Political Elite and the Class Structure' in P. Stanworth and A. Giddens *Elites and Power in British Society* Cambridge, CUP (1974) pp. 33—5

19　Dowse and Hughes *op. cit.* p. 148

20　F. and J. Wakeford 'Universities and the study of elites' in Stanworth and Giddens *op. cit.*

21　H. Glenmerster and R. Pryke 'The Contribution of the Public Schools and Oxbridge: 1 "Born to Rule" ' in Urry and Wakeford *op. cit.* p. 224

22　C. B. Otley 'Social Affiliations of the British Army Elite' in S. Van Doorn (ed.) *Armed Forces and Society* The Hague, Mouton (1970). See also T. Lupton and C. S. Wilson 'The Social Background and Connections of "Top Decision Makers" ' in Rose (ed.) *Policy-Making in Britain*

23　P. Bachrach and M. S. Baratz 'Two faces of power' *op. cit.*

24　See J. Hughes 'Nationalization and the Private Sector' in Urry and Wakeford *op. cit.* pp. 146—53

25　Y. Dror 'Muddling Through — "Science" or Inertia?' *Public Administration Review* XXIV: 3 (1964)

26　See for example Peter Worsley 'The Distribution of Power in Industrial Society' and D. Lockwood 'The Distribution of Power in Industrial Society — a comment' in Urry and Wakeford *op. cit.*

27　Worsley *op. cit.*

Index